THE
BUSINESS
OF
YOU

A Guide to Finding, Managing, and

SUCCEEDING IN YOUR CAREER

THE
BUSINESS
OF
YOU

LUKAS KRAUSE

GREENLEAF
BOOK GROUP PRESS

Published by Greenleaf Book Group Press
Austin, Texas
www.gbgpress.com

Distributed by Greenleaf Book Group

For ordering information or special discounts for bulk purchases, please contact Greenleaf Book Group at PO Box 91869, Austin, TX 78709, 512.891.6100.

Design and composition by Greenleaf Book Group
Cover design by Greenleaf Book Group
Image © AlfaroDesign. Used under license from Shutterstock.com

Publisher's Cataloging-in-Publication data is available.

Print ISBN: 978-1-62634-503-4

eBook ISBN: 978-1-62634-504-1

Part of the Tree Neutral® program, which offsets the number of trees consumed in the production and printing of this book by taking proactive steps, such as planting trees in direct proportion to the number of trees used: www.treeneutral.com

TreeNeutral

Printed in the United States of America on acid-free paper

18 19 20 21 22 23   10 9 8 7 6 5 4 3 2 1

First Edition

This book is dedicated to the friends and family who have supported me. I wouldn't be the person I am without you.

Mom and Dad, thank you for helping me believe that anything is possible. It has enriched my life beyond what words can describe.

Valerie, you are the best partner anyone could ever ask for. Tricking you into marrying me is far and away my greatest accomplishment. You are dirt worthy!

Contents

Swing for the Fences—I Did!

The inspiration for this book came many years ago, when I was beginning my career and eager to learn how to manage it. I quickly realized there was little information available on managing your career. Over the last ten years, as I was consuming information from every source possible, I started to compile notes to help create my own personal reference guide. I then started to use some of this content as I helped mentor others who were early in their careers, and I realized that this compilation of information and practices could prove helpful on a broader scale. My goal is to save you the time of compiling this information yourself and, in the process, accelerate your professional development.

As I wrote this book, I imagined the audience—you—may be someone who possesses a go-getter attitude and is looking for an edge to accelerate the attainment of your career ambitions. Or you may be an individual whose career has not progressed as you hoped, and you are looking to jump-start that career ascent.

Regardless of why you are reading this book, if your ultimate goal is to improve your performance and better position yourself for that next promotion, then you have come to the right place.

The important thing to know before jumping into this book is that managing your career is a mind-set. What would happen if you changed your focus and looked and treated your career like a business: the Business of You? Think about it. Your talents are your product, and how you operate and market yourself will determine the financial viability of that product. You are the CEO, CMO, CFO, and COO of your career. Most likely no one else will be thinking about the well-being of your business, outside of perhaps your family. The responsibility for your advancement and the management of your business rests squarely on your shoulders. That's why you need to treat your career with the strategic positioning and the tactical focus that successful businesses use, so you can maximize your talent and earning potential.

As you follow along through the chapters, we will cover key business principles and apply them to your career and its management. Some of these concepts and practices will come naturally to you and others will not. Don't neglect any of them. Make sure your strengths are built up to extend your competitive advantages while you address your weaknesses to a point where they do not hold you back.

You should consume the book in whatever way works best for you. If you are looking for a little guidance, there is a ton of practical content in the pages ahead. It would be nearly impossible to implement all of these skills and practices at once. Read through the book and grasp the key concepts. After reflection, refer back to focus on areas of interest or those in need of improvement to go deeper into the content. After achieving your objectives, graduate to another section. The content has enough depth for you to consume it multiple times.

• • •

My journey to this point started with a mind-set of improvement that I picked up pursuing my lifelong dream of playing professional baseball. Deep down, I had a firm belief that I was good enough to play at the highest level because every time I stepped onto a baseball field, I felt at home, and I experienced consistent success. But an ill-fated set of events (playing the wrong position at the wrong time, given my skills; assuming scouts would find me; not pro-actively trying to find opportunities) led to me graduating from high school without any scholarship offers. Because I didn't officially play college baseball (except for a brief stint in fall ball my senior year), I needed to develop skills and opportunities outside the normal routes to professional baseball. Without coaches, tools, or competitive games, I was forced to develop a new methodology for my development.

Over several years, I refined the methodologies for growing my talent through trial and error. In addition, I became quite adept at creating opportunities to showcase my newly developed skills. For example, I ended up with multiple private workouts with Major League Baseball teams without having much of a pedigree. This journey toward self-discovery and my consistent and intentional practice helped me fulfill my dream—I ultimately signed with the New York Mets!

This accomplishment forever changed the trajectory of my career and life. When I arrived at spring training my first year, I was in awe of the level of commitment that the other players had to developing their skill sets. Every day players worked on developing their skills. They practiced, bettered themselves, and were laser-focused on putting themselves in the best positions to succeed. Pitchers tinkered with different grips to get more movement on their pitches; hitters worked on keeping their weight back on off-speed pitches. It was all about rounding out skill sets to be as complete a player as possible.

Because of my unorthodox path to joining the professional ranks (spending several years in an office job beforehand), I was able to witness the stark contrast between the workaday office world and the constant—sometimes relentless—commitment to improvement on the ball field. As I observed my teammates' devotion to personal growth, daily practice, and intricate skill development, I couldn't help but wonder: *Why don't more people in the workplace work on honing their craft?*

After my baseball career ended and I transitioned back into the business world, I embraced a growth mind-set similar to what I'd seen embodied in my teammates. Back in an entry-level job, I was consumed by this mentality of improving my skills and output and sought out learning opportunities at every turn. I assessed my mistakes, learning from the mistakes of others, and sought out mentors. I began taking on projects that stretched me, formally and informally, and researching successful people. In a short amount of time after this hypervigilant focus on trying to find the formula behind success, it became evident to me that there are specific drivers behind those who succeed in the workforce and ways you can shortcut your path up through the ranks.

This book is focused on those drivers, and it lays out a road map for accelerating your climb up the proverbial ladder. It is chock-full of the tips and practices that helped me climb from an entry-level job to the C-Suite of an industry-leading company in less than ten years.

When I started implementing these intentional practices, my skills started to improve consistently and, more importantly, people in the organization started to view me differently. No longer was I a green employee who was not privy to discussions above his pay grade. Decision makers started to seek me out and ask my opinion on issues that would impact the organization. An interesting thing was happening: I was involved in important decisions, and I had not yet progressed very far from my initial entry-level job. This shift in how I was viewed started to create more opportunities for advancement and for both personal and professional growth. Ultimately these successes built upon themselves, and this momentum created a snowball effect on my growth.

Developing your skills while working a full-time job takes a significant commitment. But most people make the mistake of believing it takes countless hours each day to achieve any type of improvement. That daunting perception is one of the main reasons why many don't take the time to do it. Fortunately, they are wrong. Improvement takes consistent and concentrated practice—not necessarily long durations of time. Thirty concentrated, quality minutes every day will yield progress that can blow away expectations. Over time, these incremental improvements will cover a lot of ground. That is the method I have used to develop the skills that produced my rapid ascent through the professional ranks, and it is the same approach I adopted in writing this book.

The thought of writing a book initially seemed like an impossible task—especially because at the time of writing, I was running several companies and barely had the time or energy to do anything outside of work other than normal life functions. But as with the commitment I made to myself on improving my skills, I developed a schedule and cadence that I stuck to religiously so that over time I was able to produce my manuscript.

As you read through this book you will feel my passion for the content. My favorite thing in the business world is professional development. These principles and practices have changed my life, and I'm excited to share them with you in the hope that they have a similar impact on yours.

Thank you for finding my book. This book is a product of the many great people I have been blessed to know and the lessons I have picked up during my nontraditional career. I'm genuinely excited to share my insights and practices and play a small role in your achievement of your career objectives. Dream big and enjoy your journey.

IDENTIFYING THE MOST COMPELLING PATH FOR THE BUSINESS OF YOU

Everybody comes from somewhere, and some of us take rather unusual routes to get where we're going. I am often asked how a guy like me—of regular intelligence and without built-in advantages, such as family dynasty, nepotism, grooming at a young age, or elite education—could catch lightning in a bottle not once, but twice? The first time was signing with the New York Mets—at a position I had rarely played growing up. The second time was when I went from an entry-level job to the C-Suite of an industry-leading company in less than ten years.

The shortest answer to that question is: the old-fashioned way—through hard work and strategic planning. The problem is that these paths are not easily distilled down to a couple of sentences. However, if you stick with me to the end of the book, I will take you step-by-step through the practices, approaches, and strategic elements that fueled my journey.

First things first. You are a business. You produce income for you and your family. Your skills and talents are viewed as a product that employers choose to purchase through employment, choose not to purchase by extending the job offer to someone else, or worst of all, use as rationale in terminating your employment. The more valuable and desirable your talents and skills, the more likely you will have gainful employment, and the higher the price companies will pay for your services.

YOU ARE A BUSINESS. YOU PRODUCE INCOME FOR YOU AND YOUR FAMILY.

Your career and its management need to be viewed through that lens. To operate like a high-producing business, you will have a clear mission; make calculated, strategic decisions to accomplish that mission; invest time and energy toward improvement and growth; and market your business effectively.

In this section we'll walk through the business-planning process for the Business of You. We'll help you establish a clear direction on where to focus your development effort. From there, you'll fill in the framework for assessing and prioritizing your skills and development opportunities necessary to get to that next level in your career.

1

Understanding the
Business of You

You've obtained a lot of business knowledge over the years—through a combination of schooling, osmosis, or work experience. Now it's time for you to start using it to your benefit. You've been exposed every day directly and indirectly to knowledge and strategies that can be applied to your career's advantage. Starting out with a basic from Business 101, it's important that you have a firm understanding of what drives the Business of You—its strengths and its weaknesses.

The most successful businesses have a strong sense of identity and stay true to their character. They know who they are and, just as important, who they are not. It doesn't matter whether you're starting or even restarting your career journey, your success will be built upon the foundation of how well you understand yourself as a business asset. The better you understand this idea, the better you can support and position yourself for a highly productive career.

WHAT DRIVES THE BUSINESS OF YOU AND WHAT ARE THE STRENGTHS AND WEAKNESSES OF THE BUSINESS OF YOU?

Jim Collins outlined a theory in his classic book *Good to Great* in which he concludes that businesses are more likely to succeed if they focus on one thing and do it well. By doing so, they can beat their competitors and become truly great businesses. Collins's Hedgehog Concept illustrates a simple idea that flows from an understanding about what you are deeply passionate about, what you can be the best in the world at, and what most effectively drives your economic or resource engine.

Like the great businesses Collins studied over a twenty-five-year period, you can take your career from good to great by making a series of sound decisions that consistently leverage these principles.

To apply these principles to your career, you will need to start by conducting some personal assessments to know yourself better. During these personal assessments you should:

1. Find out where your preferences and passions lie.
2. Identify your strengths, weaknesses, tendencies, and skills.
3. Define your optimal work environment.
4. Understand the macro environment and trends that could impact your career path.

LOOK INWARD AND UNDERSTAND WHAT DRIVES YOU

We're all capable of performing a wide variety of different career functions. However, that doesn't mean that we *should* be performing all of them. Take me, for example: I can manage debits and credits (basic accounting activities). But the thought of being affixed to a desk crunching and organizing numbers all day makes me want to pull my hair out. I crave interpersonal interaction and love to help people learn and grow. I know that for me to be successful, my primary job functions must feed these passions.

Let's look at a serious of questions designed to initiate the process of finding out about your preferences and passions. Find a quiet place, free of distractions, and seriously think about the questions below. Take your time and think deeply about your answers. The deeper you go with each question, the closer you will get to your core feelings and preferences.

Our childhood memories provide important clues about what our consistent core values and preferences are. Ask yourself:

- What are some of my favorite memories? What activities were involved with these memories?
- What was I doing?
- Was there anyone else involved?
- Why was I so happy?
- What personal accomplishment am I most proud of?

Just like in your childhood, your educational or career experiences thus far can serve as a reference point for the types of activities and responsibilities that you enjoy and are skilled at—and vice versa. Even the worst work experiences can provide value in terms of identifying functions, environments, and activities that you would like to avoid or, at the very least, minimize in future roles. Now think back to previous roles or jobs and answer the following questions:

- In previous jobs and/or during your studies, what types of activities and responsibilities made you feel energized and made time fly?
- In previous jobs and/or during your studies, what types of things seemed to zap your energy and make time stand still?
- Looking back at your career, what accomplishments are you most proud of?

Now think about your personal time. Your choice of hobbies and how you fill your free time are great indicators of your preferences.

- What are the types of things you gravitate to in your free time?
- Why do you enjoy these activities?
- What are the elements of this activity that give you joy?
- What motivates you to pursue this hobby or activity?

You may need to repeat these exercises a couple of times to dig deep enough to find your answers. But if you take the time to answer all the questions thoughtfully, you will start to gain a better understanding of what drives you and a conscious awareness about what types of attributes your *ideal* role and work environment must possess.

ASSESSING YOUR STRENGTHS AND WEAKNESSES

Strategic leaders for top-performing businesses assess the strengths, weaknesses, and vulnerabilities of their organizations annually. There are many different frameworks out there, but one of the most commonly used is the SWOT (Strengths, Weaknesses, Opportunities, and Threats) analysis.

> The SWOT framework provides a well-rounded analysis of the key elements at play in a company that leaders need to understand in order to make informed strategic decisions.

It allows leaders to assess the organization as a whole, along with the competitive landscape, and use that information as a guiding force to drive the business in coming years.

To ensure a thorough analysis, strategic leaders collect input from internal, external, and quantitative data sources. Internal sources are those within different levels of the organization; external sources are a company's customers and suppliers; and quantitative data sources are industry statistics, customer research, and competitive research.

Take a cue from these businesses and look internally, externally, and quantitatively at your own personal "organization," so you can establish a well-rounded personal assessment that will help guide your development priorities and strategic decisions around your career. For the qualitative elements of your assessment, you will look inward for resources (in the form of conducting a self-assessment) and outward for other resources (in the form of a 360-degree review) to gain a stronger grasp of your strengths and weaknesses.

Internal assessments

First, look inward and list your strengths and weaknesses as they relate to your career pursuits. The strengths side of this list should consist of the things you do well and the activities that come easily to you. For weaknesses, think of skills and activities that are challenging for you and require additional effort and time for you to complete. Be straight with yourself. This exercise is for your benefit, so you must be brutally honest about where you are strong, as well as the areas in which you need improvement. The goal is to obtain a realistic picture from your own perspective of where you are today regarding your strengths and weaknesses. Keep this self-assessment because you will refer to it later when you are evaluating and comparing the feedback you have received from your personal and professional network.

External assessments

External feedback is the backbone of a well-balanced assessment. Collecting feedback from your manager, peers, direct reports, and friends can be an eye-opening activity, because they each have a different vantage point. If they know you well, they can give you valuable insights and round out some of your potential blind spots.

First, identify a wide-ranging mix (professional and personal) of three to five trusted individuals to provide you with an external assessment. You can use the 360 Review template in the appendix as a guide on what to send over. Prior to sending the exercise to your colleagues and friends, meet with each one personally to explain its purpose, which is to calibrate the feedback provided by each participant. Also, share that you are open to receiving direct and honest feedback because you realize that is the only way you will be able to improve. Remind them to provide specific examples whenever possible, regardless of whether they are providing praise or criticism. These specifics will help anchor you back to tangible events when you are evaluating and taking corrective measures.

THE NEGATIVE FEEDBACK MAY HURT A LITTLE AT FIRST, BUT REMEMBER THAT YOU ARE GAINING KNOWLEDGE ABOUT HOW YOU CAN IMPROVE AND GROW.

Remember to approach this process with an open mind. If you conduct it correctly, you will hear both positive and negative feedback about yourself. That's a good thing. The negative feedback may hurt a little at first, but remember that you are gaining knowledge about how you can improve and grow. Even if the feedback is delivered poorly, resist the urge to get defensive or make excuses. Instead, accept the feedback and share your appreciation to the person providing it. They offered you a gift: an additional data point. Review it objectively. Some of the feedback will be accurate and some of it will not. As you conduct this exercise more often and gain a true understanding of your skills, you will be able to quickly and accurately assess the quality of the feedback and your progress on professional development.

Quantitative data

The last element to round out your initial assessment is to use at least one of the great personality and skills assessment tools out there. These tools provide a different perspective for your analysis. Through the use of a survey mechanism, they collect data points and produce a summary of your preferences, your style for shaping your environment, and how you like to engage with others. These types of surveys have been growing in popularity lately, and the types of insights they provide add a valuable piece to a well-rounded personal evaluation. Two of my favorites among the personality profile tools are the Myers-Briggs Type Indicator (MBTI) and DiSC. Myers-Briggs and DiSC categorize your personality traits, how you engage in relationships and with teams, your psychological tendencies and preferences, and how you behaviorally shape your environment.

The last tool I recommend is the book and skills assessment from *Strengths-Finder 2.0*. This is a great book and online assessment that helps you uncover and discover your strengths. The book is packed with useful strategies on how to apply your strengths in your career.

These personality assessment tools are not guaranteed to be 100 percent accurate; however, their results have proven to be consistently strong indicators of personality traits. Even if you have a strong sense of yourself, and the results confirm a fair amount of what you already know, one of the most valuable benefits of these reports is the guidance they provide about your tendencies, how you interact with and shape your environment, and how you can be more effective in engaging with different personalities.

Think of these survey tools as a good way to round out your understanding of yourself. Even though they may have their limitations, their advantage is that they are neutral and avoid some of the biases that can come from self- and third-party reviews.

Awareness and making sense of the feedback

As you would expect, self-assessments are inherently limited because of their lack of perspective. Often we are not acutely aware of our tendencies and take our strengths for granted. That is why it's important to collect feedback from a multitude of perspectives. The external feedback and statistical analysis help to round out your evaluation to provide more of a 360-degree view of yourself.

The external feedback serves a dual purpose. First, it gives you additional data points and helps to identify opportunities for improvement that you may not be able to see by solely using a self-assessment. The other purpose is to better calibrate your *awareness* and understanding of your strengths and weaknesses. Awareness in this regard is a deep understanding of you as it relates to your preferences and strengths and weaknesses as a business entity. It means having a clear grasp of the thing or things that motivate and drive you and an honest and grounded perspective of your skill set. Awareness is an important piece in these assessments, as it allows you to be able to properly prioritize your development and to market your skill set in the workforce. Refer back to your strengths and weaknesses self-assessment and compare that list to the results you received from the colleague feedback and the quantitative assessment tools. How does it match up? If over 75 percent of the feedback matches your self-assessment, you likely already have a good grasp of your personal skill sets.

Fear not if your self-assessment did not match up well with the other feedback. Isolate the areas where there was a difference in opinion. Then, drill deeper on those items and find out why. Are they things you didn't notice until someone or one of the tools brought them to your attention? Ask yourself why you may have not noticed them personally. By acknowledging your why, you'll enhance your level of self-awareness.

Recency bias is the tendency for some people to focus on what has happened lately and weight those factors more heavily than a complete body of work when evaluating or judging something.

The quantitative assessment tools are more accurate than not, but there is always a chance they don't completely capture your essence. Before you dismiss elements of the results, think hard about those differences and see if the tools caught a characteristic or preference you did not know you had.

Looking at the differences identified

between your self-assessment and the colleague feedback, were the issues raised in the colleague feedback a one-time occurrence, or were they part of a consistent theme throughout all your feedback forms? If the issue appears to be a one-time thing, take note of the surrounding factors that could have been at play to trigger it; you'll then be better equipped to handle similar situations in the future. Finally, consider the sources providing the feedback and the tendency toward recency bias when assessing the feedback.

To get to the core of where your development opportunities reside, focus on the items that were prevalent on multiple feedback forms (meaning that multiple people identified a certain opportunity for improvement). When you look at the feedback and the specific examples provided, see if you notice any themes like the following:

- Does the behavior or tendency seem to surface during certain situations or environments—stressful times like facing a tight deadline, in meetings, Monday mornings, etc.?
- Are there any consistent triggers—other personality types or specific situations?
- Are there skills that are holding you back and/or require additional development?
- In any areas identified as weaknesses, what drove the underperformance raised by your colleagues?
  - Was it that you did not have the knowledge or experience to complete the task?
  - Or was it a lack of effort or desire to complete the task?

You should leave this exercise with an improved understanding of yourself and a couple of opportunities for professional/personal development. Note that we will use this information to chart out your game plan and development needs to deliver on your personal vision statement.

Continue to search for insights

Tap into your sources for performance information regularly. Personally, I conduct these assessments on an annual basis. Having a solid network of individuals who you can trust and are insightful is an invaluable tool. It can be difficult to get an honest and true assessment simply by surveying ourselves. Make sure to continue to cultivate these relationships and give back to them when possible, because they are providing a great gift. This is one of the major components of creating your own personal feedback loop to gauge your progress.

> HAVING A SOLID NETWORK OF INDIVIDUALS WHO YOU
> CAN TRUST AND ARE INSIGHTFUL IS AN INVALUABLE TOOL
> FOR YOUR CAREER AND PROFESSIONAL DEVELOPMENT.

YOUR IDEAL ENVIRONMENT

In his book *Outliers*, Malcolm Gladwell tackled the widespread American myth that successful people are self-made. "[They] are invariably the beneficiaries of hidden advantages and extraordinary opportunities and cultural legacies," he writes, "that allow them to learn and work hard and make sense of the world in ways others cannot."

The "hidden advantages" can be chalked up to any number of factors—socioeconomic class, teachers, parents' education level, country of birth, sex, race, and dozens more—but I think one that is overlooked in the modern workforce, especially among the most ambitious among us, is the right work environment. Putting yourself in the optimal environment for preferences and skill sets can be a huge hidden advantage.

Now, I am not suggesting that you completely steer clear of your weaknesses. I'm recommending that you put some time and energy into finding an environment that will cater to your success. When considering your career path and potential jobs, evaluate the work environment and the role itself.

Work environment: Size, culture, and mission

At its most basic level, a company can be boiled down to the size of the organization and its culture. Typically, larger companies have more structure, move at a slower pace, and have narrower roles and responsibilities than their smaller counterparts. Smaller companies tend to operate a little looser when it comes to formal procedures and bureaucracy, move faster, and have wider-spanning roles out of necessity.

These are general norms, but there are plenty of exceptions. For example, let's say that at this stage of your career you seek a wider range of responsibilities to round out your skill sets. In that case, a smaller company typically would present stronger prospects for exposing yourself to a wider range of functional experiences, because smaller companies generally do not have the same number of resources as larger companies—therefore employees are called upon to take on a wider range of responsibilities.

But on the downside, it's worth noting that the smaller company is more likely to have less stability than the larger company and also fewer advancement opportunities. In large companies, you are more likely to find opportunities to go deeper into specific disciplines and be exposed to more structure and formalized processes. As you can see, there are positives and negatives to each, but ultimately you will need to weigh these types of trade-offs with each type of company and determine which is the best fit for your given objectives.

**WHEN EVALUATING A JOB OPPORTUNITY, ASK YOURSELF
IF THE CULTURE FEELS NATURAL TO YOU.**

The other element of the work environment to consider is a company's culture. When evaluating a job opportunity, ask yourself if the culture feels natural to you. Think about it in these terms: If you walk into a large, formal consulting firm for an interview, does the formality of the environment make you uncomfortable? If so, that is a good sign that this may not be the ideal environment for you. Additionally, pay attention to the following:

- The stress level of the employees you see and meet. Are people moving around the office at a frantic pace? Does it feel like everyone has an urgent project in their hands?

- How employees interact with each other. Are they cordial or are they short and direct when communicating with each other?

- Do employees appear to enjoy themselves at work and to enjoy the company of their coworkers?

- What kinds of perks or extra benefits does the company provide? This can be a telling sign of what the company values and wants to reward. During the interview ask about the benefit packages. As an example, organizations that value talent development will often provide reimbursement for education (training and/or tuition).

Another great way to gain insights on a company's culture (or at least its desired culture) is to research the company's values, mission, and purpose. Do they speak to you? Are these targets that you can get behind? Do these align with your personal values? If you cannot find the company's values, mission, and purpose on their website, ask the interviewer. To take this a step further and understand how they are embodied by the employees, ask the interviewer how the values, mission, and purpose manifest themselves in the everyday office environment. Their response will help you see if the targets set by the leadership team are congruent with what is going on at the employee level.

In my career, I have interviewed hundreds of job candidates and worked with thousands of colleagues. In that time, I have observed that a common fatal flaw in many people's career advancement is that they are simply working in the wrong environment. No matter how talented you are, when your preferences don't align with the work environment and its pace, it ultimately undermines your ability to perform at a high level because it zaps your motivation and can warp your attitude. Don't be one of those people who discounts the importance of environment; doing so can hurt—even cripple—your career.

Identifying a shortcut

Personal awareness is the starting point for your journey. Businesses also spend significant amounts of time and resources assessing their strengths and weaknesses. The ones that thrive will look externally and examine the macro environment and their competitive environment to ensure they are best positioned for success. Likewise, you need to truly understand your strengths, your weaknesses, the optimal environment for your performance, the macro environment, and how your skills and talents fit within the broader job market. This kind of awareness can help guide your efforts and your decisions to make your climb through the corporate ranks a more efficient one.

People who participate in the stock market pay attention to what is going on with the economy to improve their decision making. It's a great way to identify strategies that will bring them value and make money. These same economic trends of the broader economy may impact your career prospects and can be used to steer yourself into business sectors that will provide you with greater opportunities.

HOW MANY PEOPLE REALLY TAKE THE TIME TO STEP BACK AND ASSESS THE LONG-TERM PROSPECTS OF A COMPANY AND THE INDUSTRY IT RESIDES IN?

Pay attention to the big trends going on around you. Is your desired industry growing or retracting? Do you think the career prospects in the taxicab industry right now are good with Uber and Lyft disrupting the space? How many people really take the time to step back and assess the long-term prospects of a company and the industry it resides in? Those who do have a distinct advantage and can steer themselves into industries and business segments with far greater opportunities.

Where do you start? A slew of economic forecasts are out there. Often they will provide starkly different predictive outlooks on what is going to happen.

My recommendation is to read several from reputable economists and governmental agencies. Additionally, pay attention to the monthly and quarterly reports (ADP jobs, housing starts, consumer confidence, etc.) for broader indicators of the health of the economy. Round out your regular consumption by visiting economically focused sites (*The Economist*, *Forbes*) and tuning to the cable business channels to stay in touch with what is going on.

By committing to the basics I've outlined, you will start to develop a foundation of knowledge on overarching trends so that eventually you'll be able to formulate your own conclusions and sniff out potential opportunities. Right now (at the time of printing) we are at an interesting time. The tech sector is white hot. Businesses today are fixated on leveraging technology to make things more accessible, convenient, and cost effective. Many people who were paying attention identified this trend early and capitalized on it through employment and entrepreneurial ventures by shifting into industries that support the sharing economy and the growing interest and economic benefits in utilizing idle assets (such as Airbnb, Uber, Lyft, etc.).

By staying on top of trends, you will be aware of and able to find opportunities in growing industries where there will be greater opportunities for employment and increased demand for your skills and experience.

IDEAS IN ACTION

- ▸ Step back and take the time to find out what makes you tick and what motivates you. These insights on your preferences, strengths, and development opportunities will serve as guiding forces in your career.

- ▸ Annually take inventory of your strengths, weaknesses, and skill sets.

- ► Taking cues from the best businesses, you should look internally, externally, and quantitatively to establish a well-rounded personal assessment.

- ► A hidden advantage is to find the best environment for you and your skills.

- ► Pay attention to the macro environment and trends to set yourself up for success.

2

Building a Vision for
Your Ideal Career

As individuals, we typically don't think in terms of charting out a career objective and building a strategy on how to obtain it—but that's a big mistake. These types of exercises are commonplace for high-achieving businesses to align efforts and track progress. Since you are in the Business of You, why wouldn't you take cues from other top-performing businesses?

Most of us do not have a clear idea of what we want to get out of our careers, so we aimlessly drift and take whatever jobs and opportunities are presented. How do you expect to get where you want to go if you don't have a desired destination? Are you just hoping that you'll stumble into your dream scenario? Good luck. Like any journey, it pays to chart out a path for how you are going to get there.

Once a year (typically in the fall), business leaders across the globe start to frame their plans for the upcoming year. They each seek to chart out a strategy and identify measurable objectives for their business. These annual plans are often designed to bring the business closer to accomplishing its vision statement. During these planning sessions, leaders must strike a delicate balance between the use of finite resources (financial and operational) and their strategic ambitions for the business within the competitive environment.

As the CEO of the Business of You, you must also chart out your annual plan and determine how to balance your available time and resources.

But before you establish your personal plan, you must develop a clear definition of where you want to end up. Your personal vision statement can serve as a guiding force to optimize your usage of your time and resources.

WHAT IS A VISION STATEMENT?

What do highly successful businesses like Google and Ikea have in common? A clearly defined vision. This vision guides their efforts and brings their team's focus to their aspirational purpose for the business's existence.

Google and Ikea, like the most successful nations, businesses, leaders, and individuals, have looked inward to understand their values, beliefs, and vision, and then striven to live by them. A clear personal vision statement is a great place to start when looking to enhance your career prospects. With this in place, you are able to focus on what is necessary to achieve your definition of success.

Here is a vision statement that has served its company well:

> Google's vision is to organize the world's information and make it universally accessible and useful.

When you read this vision statement, it is clear where Google wants to dedicate most of its time and energy. The organization has stayed disciplined and true to its vision. This focus has been one of the many driving forces behind its rapid ascension and success.

CREATE YOUR OWN PERSONAL VISION STATEMENT

Take control of your destiny by developing a personal vision statement. Your personal vision statement distills your lofty objectives into a clear and concise statement. It will set the tone for you and your pursuits. Having a well-defined purpose and destination will focus your efforts and accelerate the pursuit of your objectives.

When crafting your personal vision statement, there are two keys you need to define: personal values and core purpose.

What are your personal values (your personal brand)?

The answer to this question defines your personal brand. It's what you are promising yourself. It shows you what differentiates you from other employees. And it should guide your behavior and pursuits. Personal values can incorporate a wide range of elements. One may value personal beliefs like honesty, integrity, or kindness. Personal values also may include organizational or environmental elements, like giving back to the community or preserving the environment. It is important to understand where you stand with your strongly held values. Awareness here will help you to find opportunities that are congruent with your beliefs and fuel your efforts instead of battling internal conflicts.

What is your core purpose?

This answer reflects what your motivation for being is—and it should transcend making money. Your core purpose defines idealistically why you exist. What drives each of us is different. Here are a few examples:

- A need to feed a competitive drive
- A need to be challenged to feel fulfilled
- A relentless need to build (personal growth or projects and entities)

When you are creating your personal vision statement, you must look deep inside yourself to understand what you enjoy and what you don't. Refer back to your completed exercises from chapter 1 to identify the types of activities that make you feel energized, and the things that zap your energy or make you feel bored. These exercises will help you find the position and work environments that are ideal and the ones to avoid at all cost.

Finding roles that integrate well with your values and core purpose is key to sustaining your efforts and enthusiasm in your career pursuits.

Crafting your vision statement

Your vision statement should be grounded in practical elements; however, the challenge of the vision statement is balancing this practicality with bold ambition. So even if you're early in your career, you should be aiming very high.

Remember that this is a goal that can be measured. The goal may change over time as you evolve and gain a better grasp of yourself. Since it should be big and bold, there should be only a fifty-fifty chance that you can achieve your vision statement.

For Steve Jobs, his goal was a computer in every home. Early in my career, in my vision statement I aspired to be the president of a small-to-midsize company that drove change in creating a more enjoyable and sustainable way of life on this planet.

When developing your vision statement, think deeply about what it is you want to accomplish. Keep in mind that the more well-defined your vision statement is, the more efficient your pursuit of it will be. The most important thing to know is where you want to go. But at this stage in your career, you may not have a clear understanding of that destination or what your dream job looks like. That's OK. Just keep chipping away at it, and your end goal will become clearer over time as you better understand yourself.

Like great businesses, those people who are successful in managing their careers have a strong grasp of their skills and clearly outline what they want to accomplish. In the upcoming chapters we will help you construct a game plan for pursuing your vision statement.

CORE COMPETENCIES

Businesses use their core competencies (a defining capability or advantage) to distinguish themselves from their competitors. These skills and strengths are at the forefront in shaping a business's strategy. A perfect example is how Southwest Airlines utilized its core competencies to out-compete other airlines when it came to cost. Southwest was poised to compete on price because it had more efficient operations and a lower cost structure (no advanced seat reservations, no meals, flying only one type of plane, flying out of secondary airports and gates, etc.). This structure allowed Southwest to thrive in the marketplace with its identity as the low-cost airline, while other imitators without the same competencies floundered.

Similarly, for the Business of You, your success hinges on your ability to build your infrastructure or core competencies around your vision statement. A competency is a strength, capability, or advantage that you have in relation to others. Some examples of core competencies are strong interpersonal and social skills for sales, and creativity for marketing or design. These will serve as the foundation for success as you craft your vision statement. Playing to your strengths will lead to stronger performances and distinguishing yourself from other candidates vying for the same position.

The first step in this process is to identify the core competencies necessary to thrive in your ideal position. Secondly, conduct a gap analysis isolating the differences between where you stand today and where you need to be. The third step is to lay out your strategic game plan to develop your core competencies.

Identify the required core competencies

Shifting from long-term planning to practical day-to-day execution can be challenging. This stage of the process is that pivot point of moving from planning your long-term vision to charting out a tactical plan to get there. Converting your aspirational vision into an executable plan starts with identifying what core competencies are necessary for the role.

Look practically at your ideal role—contained in your vision statement—and isolate the key abilities required to be successful. What are the day-to-day responsibilities and demands that come with it? What are some of the skills you observe in people who excel in this role? Build a list of these key responsibilities and the skills required to thrive.

For example, let's say you aspire to be in a general manager–type role for a consulting firm. What are some of the core competencies required to successfully execute this role?

CORE COMPETENCIES FOR A GENERAL MANAGER ROLE

- Leadership Skills
  Clearly communicate and inspire teams toward the company's mission

- Management Skills
  The ability to handle the personnel challenges, professional development, and coaching, and to drive consistent performance

- Presentation Skills
  The ability to present internally (to teams and a board of directors) and pitch to customers for business development

ALSO:

- Having a well-rounded understanding of all the different parts of the business (marketing, sales, operations, accounting, and legal)

- Strong interpersonal skills, including the ability to relate and work with a wide variety of team members and customers
- Being thick-skinned and comfortable with making the tough and unpopular decisions

Most likely you will not be in a place where you are intimately familiar with the role and what it requires. Conduct your initial research by visiting job-posting sites (such as CareerBuilder, Monster, Ladders) and search for a job that best fits your vision. Take notes on what recruiters require—skills, qualifications, years and type of experience, and education. After visiting a dozen or so of these postings you should have a solid baseline understanding of what the marketplace is looking for when recruiting for this role.

Interview someone in the role

With this initial research complete, you will be prepared for a sit-down with someone who currently serves in this role. This one-on-one interview will allow you to get a much better understanding of all the elements of the position that you can't get from basic research. When trying to find a person serving in your "dream" role, start out by looking in your company. It is a great starting point, because you're able to subtly demonstrate your ambitions and create greater awareness of you and your aspirations to the higher-ups in your organization. If that doesn't work or make sense for any reason, then move on to looking in your network. Given how small the world is now, reaching out to your friends, family, and social network acquaintances (LinkedIn, Facebook, etc.) should do the trick.

When making the request to sit down with this person, use flattery to your advantage. Ask to take them out to lunch or coffee and tell them that you admire their role and would like to learn more about what it takes from someone who has been successful in it.

When you meet with this expert, your goal is to pick their brain and gain insights that only those who have sat in that chair would know. Here are the basic objectives for the interview:

- Get a clear picture of what their day-to-day looks like.
- Understand the realities of the job.
  - What aspect of the role was the most surprising to them?
  - What accomplishment in the role are they most proud of?
  - What is the most challenging part of their job?

- Understand their journey and what it took to get to this position.
- Ask about the skills used to get the role as well as the skills required for the role.
  - What skills do they use most frequently?
  - Which skills played the biggest part in getting them to where they are now?
  - What were some of their weaknesses that they have had to manage around?

Take good notes at your meeting and make sure to thank them for their time and knowledge. A nice touch is to send a thank-you email (bonus points for a handwritten note) the next day. If things go really well with your interviewee, see if they would be willing to let you shadow them for a short time. Be respectful with your request, because this is a big ask and could be a disruption to their responsibilities.

By conducting your job-description research online and meeting with a person or two in the role, you are ready to assess how your skills compare today with those necessary to achieve your vision.

Perform a competency gap analysis

To effectively pursue your vision statement, it is necessary to gain a clear understanding of how your current competencies stack up against those of your desired state. The gap analysis framework has been a valuable tool for charting out my career ambitions. It has been equally valuable when looking to improve processes or organizational outputs in the business world. A gap analysis is used to identify the difference between the current state (in this case your current skill set) and a desired future state (in this case your vision statement).

Start reviewing the list of core competencies identified from your earlier research. Go competency by competency and assess where you are today versus where you need to be. Be brutally honest when you chart out the differences between the two. Don't let the delta between your current skills and the skills you must possess for the role discourage you. With a laser focus and consistent hard work, you will surprise yourself with how far you can progress.

Let's use the example of Scott to demonstrate how to conduct a gap analysis on one's skills. Scott is early in his career and has ambitions to become a general manager or executive. During his assessments he realizes he needs to develop his presentation skills. Using the table below, Scott assesses his current state, desired future state, and several tactics to close the gap between the two.

Core Competency	Current State	Future State	Tactics to Close the Gap
Presentation Skills	• Limited experience • Lack of professional polish • Gets extremely nervous • Body language: nervous • Pacing and hand-gesturing	• Strong and confident public speaker • Conveys an executive presence when delivering presentations	• Take a presentation course • Join Toastmasters • Find opportunities to present in front of groups

Using the sample gap analysis outline, go through each of the core competencies uncovered during your research. This analysis will provide a clear idea of the development opportunities you will need to focus on to achieve your vision. From here you can begin to construct a strategy on how to develop those competencies and ultimately get the process rolling for closing in on your dream role.

Constructing your strategic plan for developing your core competencies

Once you have a clear understanding of who you are and what competencies you need to develop further, it is time to craft your goals. As Stephen Covey outlined in *The 7 Habits of Highly Effective People*, "Begin with the end in mind." This is great advice and can be applied in all aspects of your life. Strategy is something people don't often think about when mapping out their careers. Developing an end goal and a plan on how to get to your vision statement will give you a leg up on everyone else out there competing with you.

> **DEVELOPING AN END GOAL AND A PLAN ON HOW TO GET TO YOUR VISION STATEMENT WILL GIVE YOU A LEG UP ON EVERYONE ELSE OUT THERE COMPETING WITH YOU.**

When you evaluate your weaknesses, it is important to keep them in perspective. Some of these weaknesses you will need to build into strengths. Others may require you to only improve them to a point where they are not career limiters. Seek out opportunities to stretch yourself and work on these weaker areas. All too often we stick solely to our strengths and do everything we can to avoid areas where we are weak. By doing this, we are committing a disservice to ourselves. We fail to address a weak area and through avoidance can become even weaker. Don't let the fear of stumbling through something scare you away from becoming a more well-rounded individual.

With that said, do not neglect your strengths. They should be continually honed to create towering attributes that will shine and help you thrive within your career. Practice strength development as often as you practice weakness mitigation.

Strategic considerations

Equipped with the knowledge of what you need to work on, you can now focus on refining and developing those core competencies. When forming your strategy for developing them, consider the following factors in your plan:

- **Prioritize.** Determine which competency to focus on first, based on the value of the particular competency as it relates to the role. Invest accordingly to develop and sustain those higher-value skills.

- **Be Forward-Looking.** When developing your strategy for competency development, consider the long-term cycles, potential changes in technology, macro trends, and the natural evolution of your abilities. The last thing you want is to develop a skill that ultimately will become obsolete.

- **Be Action-Based.** Top performers ensure that their strategic plan is measurable and realistic.

As an example of strategic considerations in action, let's revisit Scott from earlier in the chapter. Scott has decided to prioritize developing his presentation skills because this is one of his glaring weaknesses, and in his industry, leaders make presentations often. Given that these skills are used daily to communicate to internal teams and to prospective customers, he will be able to put these skills to use right away. Additionally, Scott is relatively confident that this skill set will not become obsolete.

Unfortunately for Scott, he has very limited experience in this arena. That limited experience creates some anxiety, which manifests in nervousness and unnatural body language and hand gestures when he is presenting.

Given his limited experience and knowledge, it would be wise for Scott to start with the basics. Where could he go to build his foundational skills? With a little research online and by talking to other colleagues, Scott finds out that he has several options. His work offers reimbursement for many professional development courses, and Human Resources has provided him with a list of several that they recommend.

A strong presentation class will help Scott build the basic skills necessary to create and deliver effective presentations.

To be forward-looking, how can Scott continue to improve these skills and stay on top of different trends after his presentation course? He can accomplish this by practicing regularly and finding a source of information that specializes in this area, such as Toastmasters or other presentation organizations. He should also take advantage of every opportunity to present and polish his skills.

The last part of the strategy is being action-based. This is a great transition into how goal setting helps keep you on track as you head toward your dream job destination.

Developing an action-based plan

The old adage "What gets measured gets done" is a solid rule of thumb to apply when creating your clear and actionable plan for your development. That means precisely defining what you are looking to accomplish daily and weekly so you are able to monitor your progress every step of the way.

Using the tactics identified in your gap analysis, chart out what you are going to do in the next three, six, twelve, and thirty-six months. These goals should build upon each other. To assist with this process, I have included a goal-planning template in the appendix.

GOAL-SETTING BASICS

Whether using the template in the appendix or your own planning sheet, it is helpful to implement some of the common best practices when it comes to goal setting. Many of you may be familiar with the SMART method for developing goals, but how often do we actually apply these principles to goal setting? Here is my perspective on SMART goals.

S—Specific. Be as specific as you can with your goals. Use each one of your senses to envision the details. Create a mental picture of what your life is like when you achieve this goal:

- What are you feeling when you accomplish this goal?
- What do you see?
- What are you wearing?
- Who is with you celebrating this accomplishment?

Painting a detailed mental picture will help you to connect at a deeper level and emotionally buy into the goal.

M—Measurable. Make sure you can monitor and measure your progress toward your goal. Be very specific in what you want to accomplish so you can create a tangible set of milestones for your journey. Build a chart or visual that will help you reinforce your progress and encourage your competitive nature to update it.

A—Attainable. Your goals should be grounded in reality, but don't be afraid to go big. Dare to dream. You are the last person who should limit yourself. We all are remarkable creatures capable of more than we imagine. Often, we restrict what is possible and don't reach our full potential because we tell ourselves it is not possible. Stretch yourself.

R—Relevant. Make sure these goals are congruent with who you are, your beliefs, and your big-picture objectives. If these goals are in conflict with your cultural fabric, you will fail or tear yourself up trying to achieve this goal.

T—Time-Based. Impose deadlines on yourself. Many of us are hardwired to wait until the very last minute before starting a project. That is why aggressive timelines are important for your progress. They will help to create urgency in the pursuit of your goals as well as push you. Understand going into this process that you won't be able to control everything. Don't be deterred if you miss a deadline. Set a new timeline and focus on what you can control, like your activities and behaviors.

In addition to the SMART method, I have found that when I break large goals or tasks into "micro" tasks, I am far more effective. It helps me on multiple levels. The project doesn't seem as daunting (fighting off procrastination), and I'm able to focus in on the necessary task at hand (avoid getting distracted on a distant task or challenge).

Creating your own feedback loop

One of the best operational books out there is *Execution: The Discipline of Getting Things Done* by Lawrence Bossidy and Ram Charan. The book provides a strong framework for building an organizational culture of execution. Follow-through is one of the cornerstones of execution covered in the book. One of their examples of follow-through in practice is to never finish a meeting without clarifying what the follow-through will be, who will do it, when and how they will do it, what resources they will use, and how and when and with whom the next review will take place.

When constructing your own personal feedback loop to aid in your follow-through, there are four elements or practices to incorporate to build a strong system: Publicizing, Self-Review, Visibility, and Rewards.

PUBLICIZING

Making goals public helps build in accountability. In general, we are pain-avoidance creatures, and that tendency to steer away from pain can be leveraged when you share your goals with others. When we run into or talk to someone who knows our goals, it is likely they will ask how we are progressing with them. This helps to build the extra motivation needed for those days when it is scarce. You know the days I'm talking about. The ones where you get home from work and all you want to do is vegetate on the couch. When your goals are public, you have partners in helping you fight through that fatigue. You don't want to have to admit to them that you failed or, even worse, failed to try. Make your goals public and tap into your pride as an energy source.

One formal way to make goals public is to have a friend or loved one become your accountability buddy. Give them your plan and have them ask you about your progress. This should be a regular event. My recommendation is to do this no less than once a month. Schedule it on both of your calendars to ensure follow-through.

Additionally, if your goals are related to your current organization, it may be a good idea to share them with your manager.

Even a great manager may not be completely in tune with your personal goals. Ask for feedback on your goals and what you need to do to get that next promotion or big project. See if he or she will help you with your plan to earn it and establish a timeline. This helps you on two fronts. First, it firmly establishes your ambitions with your supervisor. Second, it memorializes the necessary action steps and time horizon for your promotion. Many managers today are in survival mode, and your promotion may not be on their radar unless you bring it up.

SELF-REVIEW

One of the most common mistakes I see is people not taking the time to assess where they are in relation to achieving their goals. Building in checkpoints and milestones will provide insights and better help you to examine what is required to cross the finish line.

Just like you set up a monthly meeting with your accountability buddy, schedule a regular assessment of your progress. Evaluate if you are ahead of schedule, on schedule, or behind. Gauge whether or not you have invested the appropriate level of effort in pursuing your goal.

VISIBILITY

In today's busy world, it is easy to get consumed or distracted with the flood of information and growing demands on our time and attention. It is helpful, therefore, to strategically place goal reminders in our everyday lives. These reminders center us and help avoid the potential to drift off to wherever the prevailing winds are blowing. Here are a couple of examples of how to effectively do this:

- Put your objectives in a highly visible place where you will be reminded of them multiple times throughout the day. I put Post-its on my monitor so that they catch my attention several times a day.
- Schedule calendar reminders. On the surface, this may sound like an obvious or insignificant tip. But it has been one of the most impactful little tricks I have found to bring me back to focus on what is important.

REWARDS

There are endless reams of research out there on the benefits of positive reinforcement. Most applications are aimed at motivating others, but the same principles can be applied to motivating ourselves.

REMEMBER, WE ARE NOT ROBOTS. EVEN SMALL REWARDS FOR SMALLER GOALS CAN HAVE A BIG IMPACT.

Think about something you have always wanted to do—maybe skydiving, or taking a trip. Make a pact with yourself that if you achieve a significant goal, you will reward yourself with this activity or experience.

Remember, we are not robots. Even small rewards for smaller goals can have a big impact.

Back to the book *Execution: The Discipline of Getting Things Done*, where the authors theorize that the leaders who are good at executing are the ones who follow through and evaluate performance religiously. I have seen firsthand

and experienced the same thing when it comes to chasing your own personal objectives. Using the tools outlined in this chapter will help you become more effective at planning and following through to achieve your goals.

IDEAS IN ACTION

- ▸ Distill your broader career objectives into a clear, concise statement. This statement will help you focus your time and energy toward the most important things for you.

- ▸ Identify the core competencies required for your desired dream role. This will help you prioritize what professional development skills to focus on.

- ▸ Conduct a gap analysis to assess the difference between your current state and where you need to be in order to accomplish the goals of your vision statement.

- ▸ When forming your plan to develop your skills, make sure it includes the strategic considerations of prioritization, being forward-looking, and being action-based.

- ▸ Leverage the SMART method when setting goals.

- ▸ The keys to a strong feedback loop are Publicizing, Self-Review, Visibility, and Rewards.

GETTING THERE: HOW TO FIND AND SECURE THAT PERFECT JOB

Those who find success in life put themselves in positions and situations where they will have a high likelihood of thriving. Many people discount the success of others and claim those people are lucky. There's a bit of truth in that, because good fortune does play a role in being successful. You must be lucky enough to be presented with opportunities and then be prepared enough to make the most of those opportunities and succeed. With some careful planning, you can strategically position yourself where you need to be. Why wouldn't you do everything in your power to be in that place? Obviously, giving yourself as many chances as possible will increase the likelihood of your success.

This plays out every day in the business world, but it is not as easy to spot when compared to how this plays out in sports. In professional team sports, athletes on a dominant or winning team are more likely to excel because of their strong supporting cast members, great coaches, and polished, proven team strategies that put the players in the best positions to succeed. While it doesn't guarantee success, the odds of the athletes on the top teams excelling are far greater than those of athletes on struggling or poorly run teams. Take this football example. The New England Patriots from 2000 through 2017 experienced unparalleled success in a sport whose governing body, the NFL, had designed rules to create parity. Year after year they bring in talented players who had previously underperformed but then ended up excelling with the Patriots. The reason many of these players experienced a career renaissance is because the New England Patriots are one of the best-run organizations in sports. They have a strong ownership group, one of the best coaches of all time, and the entire organization is committed and running in the same direction. We see this echoed in the business world, where being part of a superior team allows those team members to benefit from advantages that others do not have.

This is one of the main reasons for you to be selective in your career search. Your goal should be to seek out the types of organizations that provide you and your career with the best opportunities to succeed. For instance, look for companies, and their teams, that possess:

- A superior product or a distinct advantage in the marketplace
- A stellar reputation spanning across industries
- A supportive and collaborative culture and programs for talent development
- Management that invests in staff development and stands behind their employees

A work environment with these types of characteristics is one that will offer you an increased number of opportunities to succeed, even if others will call it luck.

As you would expect, positions at these types of organizations are more attractive to job seekers, and you will face more competition for them. In the following chapters, in addition to outlining how to evaluate job opportunities, we will walk through the basics on making yourself a far more attractive applicant to these strong companies.

3

Refining Your
"Marketing Materials"—
Resume Basics

One of a CEO's primary responsibilities is the growth and development of the organization. Investors and board members believe that if the business is not growing, it is dying. Given that you are the CEO of the Business of You, your business development efforts should be focused on seeking and obtaining gainful employment and advancing your earning potential. The best way to do that is by making yourself as attractive and marketable as possible to potential employers.

Before you can outwardly market yourself to employers, take the time to enhance your marketing materials. Your resume is your primary marketing collateral. It should be

> Business development in its most basic form is selling or identifying opportunities or partnerships/relationships to grow the business.

professional, easy to read, and concisely packaged to show what your skill set can do for this potential employer.

Job-search websites and many independent companies provide great advice and tools on developing a resume. A quick online search will yield dozens of articles, software solutions, and professional writing services to assist with the basics behind drafting a solid one. To avoid wasting time by treading over already well-covered ground, let's focus on some guiding principles for fine-tuning your professional resume that will cause it to stand out in a crowd.

Your resume, like any other effective piece of marketing collateral, must accomplish the following:

- Look professional and quickly capture the reader's attention
- Clearly define your product or service
- Speak directly to your target audience

Remember these objectives as you draft your resume. If it is executed correctly, you will put yourself in an excellent position to get to the next step in the vetting process (assuming you meet many of the minimum requirements for the position).

LOOK PROFESSIONAL AND QUICKLY CAPTURE ATTENTION

When you see an advertisement in a magazine, what do you notice? It likely captures your attention and quickly delivers a message. The designers behind these ads know that they have a brief second or two to engage the reader. The same rings true for you and your resume. Hiring managers and human resource employees are reviewing dozens if not hundreds of resumes for a given position, so it is only a matter of seconds before they decide the fate of yours. Does it make it to the follow-up pile, or is it filed away and never reviewed again?

By visiting one of the online resume building resources or consulting with your network, you will have many options to choose from for your resume template. When selecting the format, consider the following:

- Does it convey a sense of professionalism?
- How is the flow? When you read through the template, do your eyes naturally progress through the content, from section to section?

After your template decision is made you will be faced with a few design choices, including fonts and spacing. When selecting a font, stick close to the classics like Ariel, Courier, Calibri, or Times New Roman. You can get away with one of the close cousins of these fonts, but don't deviate too far and submit your resume in Comic Sans. Using an obscure font does not come across as sufficiently professional.

- Avoid the urge to jam too much information onto the page with small type size and tight spacing. Reflect back on strong advertisements and how they capture attention. The space is balanced and the content is spread throughout the entire ad, giving a feeling of symmetry.

- Do not forget to have a section dedicated to a summary of your key qualifications or skills. These days many companies screen resumes through a variety of applicant-tracking systems. The greater the concentration of relevant key words, the better the chances your resume will receive a high score and reach an actual human being. Assuming an overlap, this insertion of your key skills will help your chances of progressing to the next step in the process.

- The length of a resume should match the level of experience you have. The goal here is to balance out providing enough information to get them excited about meeting you, while leaving them wanting to learn more.

  If you are early in your career, your resume should fit on a single page. For more seasoned professionals, two pages are sufficient. Employers and recruiters are more concerned with your most recent roles and activities. If you have previous experience that adds value to your candidacy (such as a notable responsibility or company) and are having trouble limiting the length to two pages, try using a previous roles section, mentioning each one in a bullet.

COMPANIES HIGHLIGHT THE MOST GLAMOROUS AND COMPELLING ATTRIBUTES OF THEIR PRODUCTS IN ADVERTISEMENTS. YOU SHOULD DO THE SAME WHEN PRESENTING YOURSELF.

A common mistake I've witnessed from the thousands of job applicants I have reviewed is listing every single accomplishment, club, hobby, or thought on a resume to make it multiple pages. Your intent may be to impress the reviewer with your myriad of accomplishments, but this will backfire and create the exact opposite response. Do you really want the reviewer thinking about how effective you were delivering hot coffee instead of how your system refinement enhanced productivity by 12 percent? Companies highlight the most glamorous and compelling attributes of their products in advertisements. You should do the same when presenting yourself.

- Last but not least, accuracy is paramount. Imagine if you read a national advertisement, and there was a major spelling or grammatical error in the ad. What impression would be left about the company behind that ad? Employers have the same reaction when they see mistakes on a resume. They are looking for a reason to rule you out and move on to the next resume. Don't give them that chance. Proofread like crazy, and then have a friend or family member who is strong at that activity do an additional read through for you. If you don't know anyone who can help, hire a professional copy editor to review your resume. It will be the best twenty or so dollars you can spend.

YOUR PRODUCT AND SERVICES: TELL A STORY

Advertising is more than simply sharing a product or service you are selling. Effective advertising connects that product or service to what the customer needs.

It may not sound like a big difference, but that shift in mind-set can be the difference between making the sale or not. In this case the sale means getting the job. Your resume should be written in a way that allows prospective employers to have a clear vision of what you are going to do and bring to their organization.

Don't just convey information. Tell a story. The story should highlight the value you've added to previous employers and what you are capable of bringing to future ones. This story begins at the top of your resume with your career objective or summary. It is the framework of who you are as a professional, what you bring to the table, and what makes you different from the other candidates. Strong career objectives or summaries will describe what you do for employers. Here is an example of one I used on a previous resume:

> Analytical, versatile leader with in-depth experience building highly effective teams and aligning resources. Strong evaluative, decision-making, and planning skills, with a track record of streamlining processes and driving profitability. Skilled in revitalizing under-performing organizations.

When describing yourself, play up your strengths and core competencies. If you are early in your career, talk about your career aspirations. Here's another opening example:

> A creative self-starter seeking career opportunities to round out my design and management skills to grow into the position of a Creative Director.

The summary above briefly touches on strengths but quickly shifts the focus to what you are aspiring to bring to employers. Once you've started the story, it's time to reinforce what the employer is buying with proof points.

As you bullet out your responsibilities and accomplishments from previous roles or activities, use measurements whenever possible. Quantifying results helps the reviewer digest the content and adds credibility. Why do you think advertisers use stats like "30% more horsepower" or "4 out of 5 dentists approve"? Because stats work. They deliver information in a way that people are able to understand, and they quantify the impact.

An impactful structure for delivering accomplishments on your resume is to outline an action taken by you that resulted in a measurable result. For example:

> Created and implemented a system-wide incentive and engagement program that helped to drive a year-over-year improvement in franchisee growth and participation in vendor platforms by over 30 percent in each category.

When outlining your accomplishments, refer back to your summary to ensure that you are consistently reinforcing the character introduced in the beginning to avoid cognitive dissonance.

Additionally, use these accomplishments to demonstrate a wide range of skills and talents to help cast a wider net. When was the last time you heard a complaint about someone being too versatile?

Another consideration when outlining your accomplishments is to incorporate anything that can differentiate you from your competition. Is there something you did that makes you unique or jump off the page? Add it. Many of us are not comfortable with bragging about ourselves, but this is the time and place to do so.

One more tip. People typically remember the first and last statements, and tend to forget what was in the middle. A way to play that up to your advantage is to position your strongest accomplishments at the beginning and end of each section.

SPEAK DIRECTLY TO YOUR TARGET MARKET

Strong marketers spend a great deal of time, money, and energy to make certain they are speaking directly to the needs and wants of their target customers.

That way, they have the best chance of the message landing and resonating with the person who is most likely to purchase their product or service. To be more effective in landing interviews, you should follow suit.

Before submitting a resume, take a moment to consider the role and the company you are applying for. Are there certain attributes in your resume that you should play up that are most relevant? During job searches, I've used several different resume templates. I modified them to play up certain characteristics and accomplishments that would speak more directly to the different types of roles (business development, operations, training, etc.) or to the culture of the company that I was applying for. It requires a bit more work, but going that extra mile pays off when the reviewer of your resume feels like you are tailor-made for the position.

BUILDING AWARENESS

Over the last ten years, I have worked with thousands of small-business owners. The common theme among the most successful operators is a well-oiled business development engine. And at the core of that is a diverse mix of lead generation sources. That diversity helps to insulate their organizations if one lead source drops off during a given time period. Obviously, most of us are not trying to collect multiple jobs the way businesses are with customers; but harvesting multiple sources for career opportunities can help bring more openings your way and shorten the time frame between looking for a job and landing a job.

When conducting your job search, extend your reach by using all of the different job-sourcing opportunities available to you:

- Networking
- Your personal network
- Career fairs
- Placement organizations and recruiters
- LinkedIn

- Temporary and employment agencies
- Job sites like CareerBuilder, Monster, Ladders, and Craigslist
- Scanning the websites of companies you are interested in for job postings
- Joining industry organizations

Depending on the job or role you are seeking or the stage of your career, another way of finding companies that are hiring is to look for news stories and press releases (by checking cable business news stations and business websites) referencing companies that are expanding or hiring. These companies will need to find talented people to meet their expansion targets.

> *The sales cycle is the process that companies undergo when selling a product to a customer. It encompasses the work and activities associated with securing the business relationship or closing the sale.*

With a strong and targeted resume and an extremely active search effort, you will get your foot in the door with organizations. That is just the beginning of your "sales cycle." The next part of the process is interviewing and "closing the sale," or, for the Business of You, securing a job offer.

IDEAS IN ACTION

▶ Your resume is your primary marketing collateral. It should be professional, easy to read, and concisely packaged and positioned as to what your skill set can do for the potential employer.

▶ Begin with a qualifications summary or a summary of your key skills to increase the likelihood of your resume being captured with applicant-tracking software.

► Your resume should be written in a way that packages you and allows prospective employers to have a clear vision of what you are going to bring to their organization and do for them.

► Great resumes tell a story about what you have brought to previous employers and what you are going to bring to future ones.

► Before submitting a resume, take a moment to consider the role and the company you are applying for. Are there attributes in your resume that you should play up that are more relevant to this role or company?

4

Closing the Deal =
Impactful Interviews

Now that your business development efforts have paid off and landed you an interview, the real work of preparing begins. Like a business development executive getting ready for a big meeting with a prospective client, interviews are your big opportunity to land business—which, in your case, means to secure gainful employment.

PREPARE

Putting in the legwork to research and prepare for the interview can pay great dividends. The knowledge you acquire will allow you to have a deeper, more robust discussion with the interviewer; it will also boost your confidence and your ability to deliver relevant responses in clear and concise sound bites.

Your preparations can be distilled down to a few key areas of emphasis:

- The company
- The role
- The questions they are going to ask you
- Your responses
- The questions you are going to ask them

Company research

Understanding what makes a company tick will enhance your responses so they more effectively resonate with the interviewer. Additionally, you will be able to ask better questions and demonstrate your knowledge and enthusiasm for the role and direction of the company.

Start your research by visiting the company's website. Typically you'll find a wealth of information contained there. Click through the website in its entirety to understand the product or service being offered, how it is positioned in the marketplace, and how the company communicates with customers. When visiting the About Us section, take time to learn about the leadership team and the company's vision, mission, and values. They will provide insights into the organization's value structure and the type of leaders at the helm.

If you have not already done so, explore what the company's reputation is within the organization and throughout the industry. It will be helpful in gaining a better understanding of how the company services its clients and treats its employees. Some sources may contain imperfect information, so it is important to seek a wide range of sources so that your data points can blend into a well-informed view of the organization as a whole. For larger organizations, Glassdoor provides sound bites from former employees about their experience working for the organization. Yelp, Google, and other online reviews can provide similar visibility into the customer's experience. As you probably know, this information tends to slant slightly toward the negative. To make sense of it, conduct similar searches on Glassdoor and other review sites for the company's competitors to establish a baseline on performance and employee treatment. Also, leverage your network. Do you know anyone who has worked in the same industry as this company?

Finally, conduct some research on the industry as a whole. Try to find recent articles or visit industry-focused websites or publications.

After a thorough review of the company online and offline, start to think about how your responses to the potential questions the interviewer may ask can tie back to the organization's core beliefs and strategic direction. This will help you chart out ways to demonstrate your interest in the opportunity and showcase your knowledge of the business during your interview.

The role or job you want

The most basic form of preparation when interviewing for a position is to have a strong grip on what the role or job consists of, but you'd be surprised how many people don't invest the time to fully grasp it. Candidates who are ill-prepared can make incorrect assumptions or come across as less than sharp. Often they are unable to progress to a deeper level of questioning and response during the interview. This puts them in a poor position to secure the job.

A great starting point for your research on the job is to review the job description deeply. Know it from top to bottom. What are the skills that they are looking for? What are the main responsibilities? Knowing this information will help you shape and prioritize your responses to ensure they fit closely with what the employer is seeking.

Also, try to find someone to talk to who has previously served in this role or job that you want. Investigate if anyone in your network has held a similar role with another company.

Round out your research by conducting an online search of what to expect from a responsibility and compensation perspective, to prepare yourself for upcoming conversations. You'll certainly want to know what the job pays! This is relevant for any job you take on. It's helpful to have a well-informed viewpoint of what the market rate is for a given position. Compensation analysis websites will provide a salary range based on market and years of experience. Additionally they can be a solid resource for general information on the skills and responsibilities required for a given role.

Salary is typically not a "first date" or first interview topic. If it has not been brought up by the finalist stage of the process, you should initiate the conversation on benefits and compensation. Talking about money often makes people uncomfortable (even seasoned HR personnel). That is why you want to avoid bringing it up early and potentially derailing your candidacy. When the conversation does come up, be prepared with the knowledge of the market rate and what comparable pay looks like among competitors. That way, when you negotiate your salary you'll appear informed and interested in an equitable relationship, rather than appearing money hungry.

With a stronger understanding of the role and its demands, you are now far better equipped to map out the potential questions that you will be asked in your upcoming interview.

They *will* ask you . . .

The last item of research before you are ready to shift to developing and practicing your responses is to prepare for the anticipated questions that you are most likely going to be asked. This should be a standard practice for any meeting where you will be presenting yourself. Preparing for potential questions helps you to have more thoughtful responses.

Every interviewer has a different style and approach to interviewing, but there are some common questions that will surface more often than not. To prepare yourself, start with a quick online search of the top questions asked. Most of the top job sites (e.g., Monster or CareerBuilder) will have their version of the ten most-frequently asked questions. For your reference, I have included in the appendix the top questions I ask during interviews.

One way to identify potential questions is to put yourself in the shoes of the interviewer. Reference the job description as a guide to what skills and traits the company is looking for. Ask yourself what you'd want to know about a candidate you were hiring for this position. What questions would you ask to obtain the information?

Last, think back to any previous interviews you have had and what questions were asked there. Are there questions you struggled with in a previous interview? Pay special attention to those questions and add them to the top of the list for preparing your responses.

How will you respond?

With all your research in hand and a list of questions that are likely to be asked, you are ready to start constructing strong and impactful responses. First, whittle down your list to the top twenty questions, as twenty should provide a broad enough cross section of the likely questions. Prioritize the questions based on how they tie in to the role and whether they are questions you have struggled with in the past.

When creating responses to potential interview questions, take the following actions:

- List the information, preferences, approaches, and experiences that are important to convey during the interview, based on the role and what you learned about the organization from your research. Try to weave in as many of these list items as is appropriate into your responses.

- Use tangible examples from your life and work experience to demonstrate the skill or challenge conquered.

- When responding, relive whatever experience you're focusing on; don't just restate it. Pull in elements that tie in the senses (taste, touch, feel). When delivered correctly, your energy and passion will come across to the interviewer.

- Stick to the point. Get in and out of your responses quickly. This is a balancing act. You should be detailed, but don't ramble on and risk losing the interviewer's attention.

Once you have your responses prepared, practice to tighten them up. Read through them a few times and adjust as necessary. Once you have a good handle on the key points you want to emphasize, practice your responses with a friend. Give them the list of twenty questions and the freedom to throw in a few wild-card questions on the fly. Be careful not to go overboard with your practice to the point of memorizing every word of your responses. You should know the key points and the examples you want to share, but it's also important that your responses come across as natural and not overly rehearsed.

Quick tip: If you find yourself completely stumped on a question during an interview, the old trick of repeating the question is a way to buy yourself an additional few seconds. For example, if you are asked, "Tell me a time when you were confronted with a contentious situation and how you resolved it," your response could start with, "A time when I was faced with a contentious situation and the steps I took to resolve it . . . was . . . " Additionally, you could ask them a clarifying question to help you better understand what the interviewer is looking for, which also allows extra time for collecting your thoughts.

After a few practice sessions with your friend asking you your questions in a random order, your confidence will grow and you'll be almost ready for the interview.

Now it's *their* turn . . .

The last step in preparing for your interview is writing down the questions you have for the interviewer. Remember that you should be interviewing them as thoughtfully as they are interviewing you. Let's focus on the basics.

There are several types of questions that are appropriate for interviews:

- Questions on the direction of the business in the industry and in the competitive landscape. This gives you a chance to demonstrate your knowledge and research and get a feel of where this person believes the business is going. One word of caution, though, is to avoid being that person you remember from your days in school that would ask a question (if you could even call it a question) just to demonstrate to the instructor how much they knew.

- Questions that clarify any gaps in your understanding of the role and its responsibilities.

- Questions about gaining a better understanding of what success looks like. Ask the interviewer what success looks like for the role, department, and organization.

Lastly, take the time to get to know the interviewer better. Ask them something like, "What is your favorite part of working at this company?" or "What is the most challenging part of your role?"

Write down each of your questions on your notepad and take them to the interview.

Thorough prep work will help you to convey a professional, polished, and organized presence that gives you a competitive advantage in your interview. Now that this work is behind you, it is time for the fun part.

FIT IN: BUSINESS ETIQUETTE

Every environment is different, and so are the accepted norms. Think about it: Would you behave the same way you would at a sporting event like a college football game as you would at church? Of course not. By paying attention to the accepted norms of the environment, you can avoid sticking out in a negative way and demonstrate that you will fit in quickly.

When visiting a business environment, whether the purpose of the meeting is an interview or business related, it is appropriate to fit in with general business etiquette norms and tailor your behavior and dress as necessary, based on the organization.

How to dress

It all starts with what you wear. It is important that you look the part. We will delve deeper into persuasion later in the book, but one of the key principles of influencing others, from Robert Cialdini's great book *Influence: The Psychology of Persuasion,* is authority. Your appearance plays a major role in conveying a level of authority.

> **IF YOU ARE WORRIED ABOUT WHAT IS APPROPRIATE FOR YOUR INTERVIEW WITH THE COMPANY, YOU CAN ASK THE HUMAN RESOURCES REP OR HIRING MANAGER.**

Establishing your personal authority can be accomplished by wearing a professional-looking, conservative suit (and tie for men) in most settings. That's the standard. There are cases where an organization is more relaxed. I remember visiting the Googleplex for a client meeting, where I stuck out like a sore thumb in my sport coat and slacks. But no one said anything to me or even looked at me sideways. It is always better to err on the side of being overdressed, because in the opposite situation (a more formal environment), if you were dressed casually, you open the door to plenty of sideways looks and questions about your potential fit. If you are worried about what is appropriate for your interview with the company, you can ask the human resources rep or hiring manager.

Also, pay attention to the details. The interviewer is going to be examining you from every angle possible. Remember the basics—clean, pressed clothes; polished shoes; and socks or stockings without rips, tears, or holes.

Follow common sense when it comes to grooming. Your goal should be to avoid offending anyone. For men—be clean-shaven or have a well-kept beard and do not overdo it with cologne. For women—dress conservatively and don't go overboard with the perfume. Regardless of gender, make sure to freshen up your breath, so they don't remember you as the candidate with the nasty coffee breath instead of the rock star with great experience.

When to arrive

The ideal time to arrive at the reception desk is ten minutes early. When you check in, acknowledge that you are a little early. Ten minutes is the perfect balance between arriving respectfully early and not looking overanxious. Another benefit is that you won't be a nervous wreck rushing to the appointment, and it will give you time to compose yourself.

While waiting, sit patiently with strong posture. Try to avoid fidgeting or playing on your phone. If they have some trade magazines on the table, flip through them. If the company has awards on display in the lobby, view them and take note. Potentially, you'll learn something additional about the company or be able to reference one of the awards during your interview.

Why you should be gracious

The last basic element of business etiquette is that you should be gracious throughout the whole process. Smile. Be nice to everyone. I have disqualified strong candidates because they were dismissive or insensitive to the receptionist. In my opinion, it says a lot about someone (maybe they're not a team player, have a superiority complex, or they lack empathy) if they are unable to show common courtesies on a day when they are supposed to be on their best behavior.

Thank the interviewers for their time, and let them know you are looking forward to continuing the process with their specific potential career opportunity. Follow up a couple of days later with a thank-you email or—if you want bonus points—a handwritten thank-you letter. It shows your gratitude, and it serves as a friendly reminder that you are an interested and thoughtful candidate.

Interviewers and hiring managers are more likely to move forward with the qualified candidates they like and feel they will be able to work with comfortably. Follow the basics of general etiquette and friendliness and you'll give yourself a stronger chance of securing the position you want.

That certain something: Presence

Depending on what study you read, you will see varying percentages (some say upward of 90 percent) that suggest that the largest part of any given message comes from nonverbals (such as posture and facial expressions). What are you saying with how you carry yourself? With just a couple of tweaks to your posture and body language, you can portray a professional and confident presence during your interviews.

WHAT ARE YOU SAYING WITH HOW YOU CARRY YOURSELF?

Let's start out with the basics on what you can do to give off that important positive impression.

Start off on the right foot by greeting the receptionist upon your arrival with a smile and a warm acknowledgement. While waiting, practice good posture by standing up straight and taking a wide stance (slightly wider than shoulder width). Good posture and occupying more space can help you feel and convey confidence. Similarly, if you are waiting in a chair, make sure to sit up straight.

Once the hiring manager or human resources team member comes to get you, stand up if you're seated, put a little bounce in your step, make eye contact, smile, and greet them with a firm handshake. Humans are hardwired to make snap decisions and size others up immediately, so make sure to start off right by delivering a positive first impression—that you are a friendly, energetic candidate.

When you sit down for the interview, find a comfortable position to settle into. Feeling comfortable will help to calm any nerves that you may have. Just remember to carry yourself with confidence. Here are a few pointers:

- Maintain a strong posture: Keep your shoulders back and your chin up.

- Make eye contact with the interviewer for the majority of the time you are responding (let's say 75 percent of the time). Find a comfortable focus and pay attention without giving a constant, unblinking stare that makes the other person feel uncomfortable.

- Avoid fidgeting, so you don't give off the impression that you are nervous or not being completely truthful.

- Make sure your hands are visible and not "hiding" below the table. This may sound like a strange tip, but again, it's something that has been coded into our brains over time (most likely as a protective mechanism). We think there is potential danger or someone is trying to hide something when we can't see someone's hands.

- Speak up and deliver your answers with energy and conviction.

If these presence basics don't feel comfortable, practice them leading up to the interview to help them feel more normal for you. Using these tactics in everyday situations, like at the dinner table, will help you ease into a greater level of comfort, with these minor adjustments to your body language. Once they feel natural to you, you will not only *feel* more confident, but you will ultimately come across as more confident and competent to interviewers.

Questions to Ask the Hiring Manager

- In most cases, at the tail end of the interview the interviewer will give you a chance to ask questions. In addition to the questions you prepared, it is valuable for you to gain a better understanding of who you may potentially be working for. Here is a list of some questions to consider asking your potential new boss:

- How long has the hiring manager been in this position?
- What is the hiring manager's record for promoting staff? This should be asked more indirectly. What is the typical path of a successful _____ (fill in the blank with the position you are interviewing for)?
- How does the hiring manager handle professional development and providing feedback?
- How does the hiring manager handle coaching and development opportunities?
- What is the manager's philosophy on recognizing employees?
- How does the manager handle stressful situations?
- What is the manager's approach to handling conflict?
- What is the manager's communication style?
- What types of things would former and current employees say about working for the manager?

Questions to Ask Team Members (if you are allowed access during the screening process)

- If you are given the opportunity to interview potential peers or team members who work for the hiring manager, this will provide an excellent chance to learn more about your potential new boss and the company from a perspective that is comparable to your own. Here are a few questions to ask:
  - What is their favorite and least favorite aspect about working for the company?

- What is their favorite and least favorite thing about working for this manager?
- How would you describe the management style of the manager?
- How does the manager engage subordinates with professional development?
- What is the manager's philosophy on recognizing employees?
- Specifically, what has the manager done to help you achieve your objectives and advance your career?

AFTER THE SHOW

High performers, whether in sports or the business world, take advantage of every opportunity to improve and refine their skills. World-class athletes and coaches spend countless hours going over film or replaying past performances and practices in their minds to enhance their future performances. Unfortunately, you don't have the luxury of recording your interviews (although you can record your practice sessions), but that doesn't mean you are not able to extract the same benefits that professional athletes and coaches do.

After the interview, step back and reflect on your performance. For best results, try to conduct your reflection as quickly as possible (within a couple of hours). Replay the interview step by step in your mind. Take inventory of when you felt effective and the words flowed naturally. Pinpoint why you felt this way. Also think back and identify which responses seemed to resonate with the interviewer (times where they leaned in toward you or praised you).

On the opportunities-for-improvement side, which questions did you seem to struggle with? Take note of those questions and work on your responses to them. What responses had a different effect than you intended? Why do you think they went that way? Do you need to tighten up your phrasing on those responses, or did they open up a different topic and veer the conversation into an undesirable place?

With this feedback in hand, you are well equipped to enhance your personal authority for future interviews. And if you can subscribe to a mind-set focused on continual improvement, you will make remarkable strides and increase your likelihood of success exponentially.

Remember to take the time to do your research and prepare for your interview. It takes work and isn't very glamorous, which is why many candidates fail in this area. But doing thorough research and preparation is one of the easiest ways for you stand out in a positive manner.

IDEAS IN ACTION

- ▶ When preparing for an interview, focus in on these key areas: the company, the role, the questions they are going to ask you, your responses, and the questions you are going to ask them.

- ▶ When responding, use tangible examples from your work experiences and relive the experience with passion and energy; don't just restate it. Pull in elements that tie in the senses.

- ▶ Be gracious to everyone you encounter throughout the whole recruitment process.

- ▶ Humans are hardwired to make snap decisions and size others up immediately. Make sure to start off right by delivering a positive first impression—as a friendly, energetic candidate.

5

Should You Accept?

When you accept a job offer, it is like entering into a strategic relationship with an employer. Prior to entering similar types of arrangements, business executives spend a fair amount of time researching, assessing, and vetting the potential partnership to ensure they are the right fit for the organization's long-term aspirations. A solid practice when evaluating strategic partnerships is to compile a scorecard that weighs the positive and negative attributes of each partner. This provides a more tangible and systematic approach to the evaluation process, and keeps you from simply making gut decisions that get rationalized after the decision is made. You should conduct the same type of evaluation and examine your potential career opportunities from every angle. Your personal scorecard should link back to your vision statement. Also, it will likely include categories like advancement opportunities, organization reputation, skills development, environment, and company culture.

Accepting an employment opportunity is a major decision. It can be a long-term relationship that can strengthen or hamper your career ascent. Often job seekers are somewhat cavalier with their review and assessment of a job opportunity. The goal of the job seeker is to find and secure a job; so when presented with an offer, many will quickly pounce on that opportunity with little thought or assessment. This is a big mistake, because they could be putting themselves in a damaging position. There are two main reasons job seekers do this: fear and laziness.

People are afraid of missing out on a seat in the game of employment musical chairs. This fear can have some merit and should be considered, especially if your financial position is tight. But this fear should not consume you and dictate that you accept a weak opportunity.

The second condition, laziness, occurs because it's easier not to do the legwork and the homework. Skipping the assessment of the opportunity out of ease is foolish. Working for the right people, in the right opportunity, can supercharge your development and make an immense difference in your career prospects. Demonstrate some discipline here, and you will put yourself in a far better position to succeed compared to your peers in the long run.

It pays to think two steps ahead when it comes to your career. By evaluating opportunities from all angles, you'll be putting yourself in the best position to achieve your goals. Three key areas you should examine when considering a job opportunity are the company, the hiring manger, and the role.

EVALUATE THE COMPANY

Throughout your career, it is important to make sound decisions about where you work and who you work for. A common mistake people make is focusing solely on the role in front of them when considering opportunities. By doing this you run the risk of ending up working for a sub-par manager or a company that chews up and spits out employees. Ideally, you want to put yourself in an optimal environment to give yourself the highest likelihood of success. That means finding the positions that will develop you and provide ample opportunities for you to grow and advance.

KEEP IN MIND THAT THERE ARE TIMES WHEN THE COMPANY YOU WORK FOR IS EVEN MORE IMPORTANT THAN THE ACTUAL ROLE YOU HAVE BECAUSE OF WHAT THAT COMPANY CAN DO FOR YOUR CAREER.

Sometimes success is as simple as avoiding toxic situations by spending a little extra time and energy to identify some key red flags. Keep in mind that there are times when the company you work for is even more important than the actual role you have because of what that company can do for your career. If the company has a sterling reputation and is an organization that trains and develops great talent, it can propel your advancement in future roles outside the company. But in most cases, the quality of the company is just one of many factors you weigh when deciding on a new job opportunity.

The following are key scorecard items to consider when evaluating a potential company to partner with. As you will notice, there is some overlap from your initial research on the company that will either be solidified or altered, based on your experience in the interview process.

- Start by looking at how the company is viewed in its industry and in the broader economy as a whole.

    Step back and honestly evaluate the business's reputation from a holistic perspective. Is it viewed as a leader or a follower in the industry? How would it look to have this company's name on your resume? This weighs heavily in the development of your personal brand. For example, the Big Four accounting firms have a reputation for snagging the top-level college recruit talent and developing strong performers. Individuals who have spent time in those firms are viewed as potentially strong candidates when they go through subsequent interview processes. Because of the reputation of the talent those firms attract, their training, and their work ethic (they have been known to work employees hard, especially when audit season rolls around), when these individuals leave the consulting world, companies are often quick to hire them.

- What size is the company?

In most cases, large companies (more than 500 employees) have a dramatically different work environment than smaller companies. Most large companies tend to have clearly defined structures and work parameters. These companies typically have a proven track record and have developed mature checks and balances based on their experience. In contrast, most small companies have a looser structure and less red tape. Generally, smaller companies can be more nimble. Their flexible environment puts heightened pressure on managers to guide and lead, though, as they don't have the well-defined rules and guidelines of larger companies.

Larger companies, in most instances, provide greater stability and resume credibility. In smaller companies, you're likely to be called upon to take on responsibilities outside of your job scope and have opportunities to be exposed to other areas of the business. Often a smaller company presents chances for you to develop a wider range of skills and experiences. These opportunities can present a higher risk; however, they can also deliver a higher reward and quicker advancement, as it can be easier to stand out in a smaller organization.

- Determine what direction the business is heading in.

Is it growing or retracting? Growing organizations often have more opportunities for advancement because they are fighting hard to keep up with their growth and staffing needs. I have sought out these types of companies in my career, because they offered me a chance to make my mark, have an impact, and grow along with the company. Also, in my opinion, the positive energy that radiates from an organization that believes it can change their industry is fun, if not intoxicating.

- Does the organization promote from within or recruit outside talent for staffing needs?

  This will help you determine what kind of advancement opportunities you will have with this company. It doesn't mean you should immediately rule out a company if it doesn't have a reputation for promoting from within. It's worth taking into consideration, though, that it may not be a long-term employment play for you if you wish to climb through the ranks.

- Get to know the corporate culture.

  The culture should align well with your beliefs so that you don't constantly get frustrated over the direction and decisions made by the business leaders. There are several vehicles you can use to collect this kind of information. Refer back to your notes from your interview process for indicators of the culture.

These data points, along with your initial research (Glassdoor, online reviews, and meeting with former or current employees), should provide you with a solid picture of the organization as a whole and how it fits within your objectives.

EVALUATE THE MANAGER

When evaluating the role, learn as much about the hiring manager as you can. To me, this is one of the most important things to consider. The key is to find a strong leader who will assist you in cultivating your talents and provide you with opportunities to showcase your skills. Choose wisely, because I have seen many talented people stall out their career development underneath a weak manager.

When you go through the interview process, you will normally meet and have the chance to assess the hiring manager—your potential new boss. Ask if it is possible to meet with direct reports, team members in this current role, or other team members to get a broad perspective of the working dynamics and culture. Interview them about the work environment and the values and tendencies of the hiring manager.

If you meet with direct reports, you will need to dig deep to unearth negative themes (if they exist), because it is highly unlikely that a direct report will come straight out and say that the manager is terrible, or a jerk.

Consider the following when assessing the quality of hiring managers:

- **Organizational Clout.** How is the manager viewed within the organization? Is this manager a person who carries a lot of authority? Under a strong manager with clout, you are more likely to benefit by receiving higher visibility, more resources, and more advancement opportunities.

- **Their Motivation.** Is the hiring manager fixated on his or her own advancement ambitions, or is the manager a professional who develops talent? Be cautious of the former, because you may get stuck under a glory hog or a chess player who is interested solely in advancing his or her own ambitions.

Think back to some of your best managers, teachers, and coaches and how they impacted your progress and development. It's likely they did many of the following for you and your career:

- Created an environment that best positioned you to thrive
- Removed obstacles that you encountered along the way
- Mentored and developed your strengths along with your weaknesses
- Advocated for you and your advancement
- Provided honest and useful feedback
- Inspired you to push beyond what you believed you were capable of accomplishing

Managers who consistently do these things are the ones you should align yourself with. They will build you up and help you achieve your career objectives. Managers with this skill set and mind-set are not abundant. Throughout your career you will need to search for these types of managers and strategically align yourself with them. They can be a secret advantage that will help to propel your career.

Interviewing the manager

During the interview process, it's important to ask the hiring manager certain questions. Remember to utilize the questions outlined in the previous chapter to gain a better understanding of who the hiring manager is. By observing how they respond and by interviewing direct reports (if possible), you'll gain a better grasp of their abilities, style, influence within the organization, and motivators.

When getting to know the hiring manger, the purpose of your questioning is to better understand:

- Their priorities and personal ambitions
- Their approach and philosophy to the professional development of staff
- How their role and yours fit into the broader organizational initiatives

When you reflect on your interview, pay special attention to how the hiring manager responded to the questions. How did he or she describe and emphasize (or downplay) specific elements when responding to your questions? During the interview, look for subtle indicators like responding with enthusiasm (or the opposite), or what topics they struggle to form a thoughtful response to. For example, if you were to ask a hiring manager about their philosophy on and approach to professional development, and they stammer through a hollow response without any tangible examples of what they value, it's likely a strong indicator that they spend very little time and energy on formally developing their direct reports.

Also, recall how the manager interacted with other team members and vice versa. What did the exchange between the manager and the receptionist look like when the manager came to get you for the interview? Was it cordial and warm, or did the manager fail to even acknowledge the person?

A good tell on genuineness is how a person treats those who cannot do anything for him or her. The same goes for assessing their interactions with team members. Does it seem like there is genuine respect (both ways)? Watching how team members respond when they cross paths with the hiring manager can tell you a lot about how they view the manager.

The warning signs: Avoiding a weak manager

During the interview process, you should be interviewing the company as much as the company is interviewing you. Take notes. When you are collecting information, be on the lookout for potential warning signs that suggest that the hiring manager (your potential new boss) may not provide an optimal environment for you:

- The hiring manager spent more time talking about his or her own accomplishments and track record than that of the team and the organization.
- The hiring manager talked far more than you did in the interview. You left the interview feeling like you had to fight to get a word in.
- The hiring manager came across as disinterested in the process and learning about your skills.
- When the manager talked about team or department accomplishments, there were disproportionately more "I's" and "me's" than "we's" and "us."
- When you asked questions of the hiring manager (or a team member talking about the hiring manager), did the responder:
  - Hesitate before answering?
  - Look around before responding candidly?
  - Avoid certain topics by answering a different question?

- Listen closely to hear what was not said during their response.

WEAK MANAGERS

Bad managers are career kryptonite. Unfortunately, most of us are likely to end up working for a weak—or even aggressively bad—manager and may not know it at first. It happens because we are engrossed in our daily responsibilities, lack perspective due to being too close to the problem, or have no reference point or awareness of what we should expect from a manager. Here are some of the common archetypes of weak managers.

The Micro Manager—Hovers over you constantly and wants to be overly involved in every tiny decision and element of your work. This manager's "go-to moves" might be checking in umpteen times a day for updates or wanting to be cc'd on every email, no matter how insignificant. This lack of autonomy ends up being a large impediment to your overall effectiveness and, frankly, is exhausting to deal with.

The Glory Hog—Takes credit for everything positive that is happening. After a big team success, the Glory Hog, even without adding noticeable value, is quick to swoop in and marginalize the credit given to others for their contributions. This manager uses "I" and "me" instead of "us" and "we." Also, Glory Hogs are typically quick to point fingers and pass blame if something goes wrong.

A Whole Lot of Sizzle, but Very Little Steak—Talks a giant game about all they are doing, but contributes next to nothing to the overall success of the team and organization. A close cousin to the Glory Hog, this manager plays up his or her role in the completion of daily activities and successes. The inefficiencies in the organization have allowed this character to skate and climb up the ranks simply by being a blowhard.

The Politician—Have you ever had a manager or coworker with whom you had to choose your words very carefully because you knew that they would likely twist them and ultimately find a way to use them to their personal advantage? Meet the Politician. This manager spends most of their working hours angling for other positions, gossiping, slinging mud, and engaging in office politics. With every interaction, the Politician tries to find an angle to exploit for professional gain. It is extremely difficult to get things done or understand the ulterior motives when working with this person.

The Know-It-All—Accepts no input from anyone. Team meetings and discussions feel like a formality, solely as a means for the manager to demonstrate that he or she is the smartest person in the room (which usually is not the case). This manager is also unwilling to acknowledge missteps.

The Pretender—Is underqualified for the role. Chaos ensues around this manager as problems "boil over" because nothing gets handled properly. The team pays a heavy price because of the Pretender's ineptness.

The People Pleaser—Lacks the backbone necessary to lead. People Pleasers have a hard time holding team members accountable because they are preoccupied with trying to be liked by everyone.

Ideally, you will be able to sniff out a bad manager before accepting a new role; but even after doing a thorough review, you may not be able to spot one. Regardless, take the time to conduct your assessment to increase your chances of aligning with a strong manager—someone who will help propel your professional growth.

HOLDING OUT FOR GREENER PASTURES

In the past, I have passed up promotion opportunities because of the hiring manager. In one instance, it was quite evident that the manager was not a leader. This manager had a track record of being self-serving and building his reputation off the backs of his direct reports. He had no experience leading teams and had come straight from the consulting world. At the time, my coworkers thought I was crazy for passing up the opportunity to work for this up-and-comer.

I turned down the promotion in a professional manner to avoid burning bridges. In the end, things worked out for the best. Two months later an even better opportunity with a stronger manager presented itself. In two short years the weaker manager's career flamed out (within the organization) because he was unable to generate results due to his lack of management skills. He was demoted. Those working for him did not have a great fate, either—his direct reports lost their jobs.

Vetting a manager is not an exact science, and a red flag or two should not completely disqualify a job opportunity; but being observant can help reduce the risk of working under a weak manager. Bad managers make your job more difficult than it already is.

Be strategic: Decide with your brain, not your gut

Evaluating the merit of a potential job opportunity is one of the most under-appreciated skills. All too often people become enamored with the idea of a job because of a single element and then rationalize to themselves why the role is the right fit for them. Salary, title, or a company's name are sometimes all it takes to lure a job seeker. I am not saying those things are unimportant, but rather that you should take a comprehensive view when considering your next move, so you can make a well-informed decision, not an emotional one.

> **IT IS COMMON FOR YOUNG PROFESSIONALS TO DISMISS A ROLE BECAUSE IT IS NOT THEIR DREAM JOB OR THE CONVENTIONAL ROUTE TO THEIR DREAM JOB.**

Before accepting a new job, examine how the role fits into your broader career objectives. It is common for young professionals to dismiss a role because it is not their dream job or the conventional route to their dream job. Throughout this journey there will be times when a calculated sacrifice is necessary for future gain and growth.

A solid starting point for a well-rounded assessment of the quality of a position is to evaluate it from three fronts: Enjoyment, Development, and Strategic Advantages.

YOU SHOULD ENJOY IT

Every job and role will have elements that are not enjoyable. This remains true at all levels within an organization. Even as the CEO of a company, there are still aspects of my job that are undesirable. When analyzing potential role enjoyment, focus on how you will spend most of your time and efforts. What does the average day look like? If thinking about those day-to-day rigors makes you cringe more than smile, you may have a problem with enjoyment.

Another consideration is how well the responsibilities line up with your skill sets. If you will be in over your head, you will likely not enjoy the role, and you also may not last long in the role. Take a moment to reflect on the demands of the role—skills required, daily responsibilities, customer-facing versus non-facing, and the level and type of conflict you will encounter (with customers or office politics) and your abilities to manage them on a regular basis. Every role will require you to learn and grow; just make sure you are not jumping into a position that could stretch you to the breaking point.

The last cautionary tale to watch out for is the no-win situation. This is not always easy to sniff out. Once I was presented with one of these, and fortunately for me, it was glaringly obvious that I was being set up to fail. I was offered a position to run a division, but they wanted me to double our growth numbers from the previous year while cutting the staff in half. It didn't take a genius to figure out that this was a nearly impossible task, and I declined the role. The individual who ended up taking the job did not hit the growth targets and was unceremoniously let go less than a year later, ultimately branded as the fall guy for this "failure."

If you are early in your career, a no-win situation could be one where there has been high turnover in the position you are being considered for and your research (interview process, Glassdoor, talking to employees you know in your network) shows that you will not be given the support and resources necessary to succeed. The company is looking for a miracle worker, and you have almost no margin for error.

It is important to recognize that there will be situations when you will need to take a role you may not enjoy in order to serve a greater strategic purpose (and I have done that on multiple occasions). Know in advance that doing activities that you do not enjoy will wear you down over time; so if you do proceed with one of these roles where most of your daily activities are less than desirable, make sure that you have a defined timeline and consider how you will benefit from this delayed gratification. It probably would not hurt to plan on finding joy in other places while you grind through this "paying your dues" role.

YOU SHOULD BE ABLE TO GROW

The next aspect to consider is how the role fits into your personal and professional development. Ideally, a role will help you develop your skills and prepare you for the next level of responsibility. When evaluating your opportunities, seek out roles that:

- Provide a strong onboarding/training process that prepares you for your responsibilities
- Give you a chance to further expand the skills necessary for your vision-statement role
- Present you with opportunities to develop new marketable skills
- Serve as an informal prerequisite for your planned career track (for example, if you were to run a multiunit operation, first you will have to run and demonstrate an expertise at operating a single operation)

Be selfish when it comes to your development. Finding companies that value this does not change the fact that it is your responsibility. Your employer should expect a lot out of you, but you should expect to get a lot out of them while performing in your role.

WHERE WILL IT TAKE ME?

The last front to evaluate includes the strategic advantages that may come with a given role versus other positions. These advantages should not be a trump card that outweighs other considerations. They should be one of many elements considered, and they're more likely to serve as a tie-breaker if you are evaluating multiple strong opportunities. Some common examples of strategic advantages are:

- Access to and interaction with key team members that you can learn from and who will be influential in your advancement
- Having a title or an employer that has weight within the industry
- Being part of a team or project that is the "big" initiative for the organization or relates directly to experience that you need for your vision statement

If you are an internal candidate considering a different role within the organization you currently work in, you will have some additional insights that an external candidate will likely not have access to. As an internal candidate, consider the following factors:

- How is the role viewed within the organization?
- Does the role and/or department have any special strategic importance to the company and its objectives? When this is the case, you are in a higher-visibility position and have more opportunities to shine in the eyes of key decision makers within the organization.
- What is the history of this department and what is its reputation? Is it growing or is it retracting?

These strategic advantages can pay nice dividends by creating a larger platform for you to thrive and ultimately accelerate your climb through the ranks. It is worth taking these factors into account when assessing the positives and potential drawbacks of a given position.

Unfortunately, there are no perfect roles, with perfect bosses, within perfect organizations. But if you contemplate all of the previous information, you will be able to evaluate each opportunity in a systematic manner and make an informed decision on what role best serves your career aspirations.

UNFORTUNATELY, THERE ARE NO PERFECT ROLES, WITH PERFECT BOSSES, WITHIN PERFECT ORGANIZATIONS.

Successful businesses spend significant resources analyzing the customer, the competitive landscape, and their internal operations to put themselves in an optimal position to succeed. This analysis that businesses conduct is not an exact science, and neither is your analysis of a potential employer and employment situation. That is why it is paramount to collect as many pieces of information and data points as possible to build out your scorecard to improve your chances of making the right decision.

After you review each strategic factor, pull together your research and notes to assess how the company, manager, and role fit in with your career objectives. One way to compile your results in an organized and logical format is to use a balanced scorecard. A balanced scorecard is a planning and management tool designed to assess and rank how well a situation or business decision aligns with the vision and strategy of the organization. This performance measurement framework was originated by Robert Kaplan and David Norton, first in a *Harvard Business Review* article and later in several books.

Your equivalent of a balanced scorecard assessment of a job opportunity can be built by scoring each job opportunity on a scale of 1 to 5 for the areas you identified as important based on your career objectives, in addition to factors outlined in this chapter. The opportunities with the highest score are closer matches for your personal plan. Adding this kind of quantitative measurement will help you assess each opportunity more pragmatically than if you rely on your gut.

From there, plan your next steps to pursue the opportunities that best fit into your plans. And don't forget to send your thank-you cards.

IDEAS IN ACTION

▶ Accepting a new job is a major decision. It can be a long-term relationship that can strengthen or hamper your career ascent, so take the time to vet each potential employment opportunity.

▶ The three key areas to examine when evaluating a job opportunity are: the company, the hiring manger, and the role.

▶ The quality of your direct manager is one of the most important things to consider when evaluating a new role. The key is to find a strong leader who will help you cultivate your talents and provide you with opportunities to showcase your skills.

▶ Unfortunately, there are no perfect roles, with perfect bosses, within perfect organizations. But if you explore all of the information from this chapter, you will be able to evaluate each opportunity in a systematic manner and make an informed decision on what role best serves your career aspirations.

ESTABLISHING YOUR COMPETITIVE ADVANTAGE: HOW TO OUTPERFORM THE COMPETITION

Michael Porter, in his book *Competitive Strategy*, defines competitive advantage as a business concept that describes the attributes of an organization that allow it to outperform its competitors.

Businesses spend countless hours and resources developing their strategic advantages. Thriving businesses cultivate and maintain these advantages so they become part of the corporate identity. These advantages can come in all shapes and sizes, but many of them grow out of these three common traits: a dynamic corporate culture; superior talent development; and operational efficiencies.

As we work on the Business of You, we are going to use these themes as a launching pad to go deeper into the personal applications of harnessing a dynamic personal culture, optimizing your environment to develop your skills and talents, and maximizing your daily output.

The following chapters are aimed at providing you with a major leg up on your competition by refining your skills and increasing your daily capacity.

6

Harnessing a
Dynamic Personal Culture:
It's All about Attitude

The culture of an organization has the power to inspire employees to move mountains and to support each other in a way that, when executed correctly, creates one of the most defendable competitive advantages of all.

Take Zappos, for example. They provide a service (online shoe shopping and recently expanded into other apparel) that is rather commoditized and not overly extraordinary. However, they have been wildly successful and disrupted their industry. The backbone to Zappos's success is an amazing culture that creates a world-class

> Disruption in the business world uproots and changes how an industry behaves, how it does business, and how customers consume the product or service.

customer experience able to breed loyalty. This has driven remarkable growth through word-of-mouth marketing.

Winning cultures in the business world are those in which team members share a purpose through a clear vision and set of values, are committed to learning and growing, trust each other, and communicate effectively.

A strong personal culture can have a similar effect on your career. With a dynamic personal culture, you can continually improve and harness a built-in advantage over others vying for the same roles. You will be able to generate more output through a consistent approach to conquering your daily responsibilities, in addition to being viewed internally as an ambitious team player.

> ### THOSE WHO EXCEL IN THE WORKPLACE MASTER
> ### THE MANAGEMENT OF THEIR ATTITUDE.

You have already established your purpose by following the steps laid out in the earlier chapters of this book. For your personal culture, your attitude is the underlying driver. A strong, positive attitude will propel your performance each day and weigh heavily on how you are viewed within your organization. Those who excel in the workplace master the management of their attitude. Top performers with a strong personal culture bring positivity and consistently exude confidence—while embodying ownership in everything they do.

ATTITUDE AND PERCEPTION: A TWO-WAY STREET

A positive and collaborative culture is a pillar of highly productive businesses. Companies will dedicate significant resources to foster an environment that supports this kind of culture. Their efforts consist of conducting regular employee satisfaction surveys, recognition programs, formalized social events, team-building activities, and even strategically configuring the office space, all aimed at building a positive culture.

You should make similar investments of time and energy to enhance your own personal organization's culture—the attitude you bring to the office every day. As you start to pay attention to your attitude, it will become abundantly clear that it is a major driver in your output. Think back over the last two weeks and isolate the days where you were most and least effective. Why do you think that is? If you dig deep enough, you may find that you were in a great mood on the productive days and had something that derailed your mood on the less-than-productive days.

Another important way attitude plays a role in your success is how you interact with and are perceived by other team members. Like it or not, perception plays a major role in important employment decisions (like transfers and promotions). How you are perceived within your organization could ultimately help or hurt your chances of being awarded the next "big project" or advancing up the ranks. Even in today's tech-driven business world, business is still a people sport. Your performance is important, but if you are difficult to work with, you'll be held back. People want to work with team members they can get along with. It also helps if that person is an eager go-getter who is willing to jump in and help rather than not carry their weight.

Think about it in this way: At times, the workplace can be like a desert island (a confined space where you are stuck with people). In each case, a group of people works toward a common goal—on the desert island it is to survive, and in the workplace it is to meet the company's objectives. If you were stranded on this hypothetical desert island, choose which of these people you would prefer to be stranded with:

- The griper who complains about everything and is unwilling to jump in to help the team, or
- The self-starter who is always positive and willing to lend a helping hand.

Most of you would select the self-starter. First and foremost, the self-starter will be willing to do whatever it takes to help survive. And for less functional reasons, it's likely that the griper's defeatist attitude will eventually annoy you, bringing you down and impacting your ability to survive.

**WE ALL HAVE DAYS WHEN WE ARE
NOT OURSELVES, AND THAT IS OK.**

Given the impact attitude has on your day, we should do our best to manage it effectively. Become more mindful of the attitude you project daily. We all have days when we are not ourselves, and that is OK. The key is to work on this skill (and yes, your attitude is a skill that you can improve on) to increase the number of days where attitude is up rather than down. Let's look at a couple of different strategies to cultivate a positive attitude.

Starting off on the right foot

Have you ever noticed that when your day starts off with some good news, then the rest of the day often follows suit? It would be great if we could manufacture good news every morning, but we know that is not realistic. What you can create is a morning routine that starts you off on a positive trajectory.

This strategy is centered around designing your own success routine to start your day off right—putting yourself in the best position to have a positive and productive day. This is possible by creating emotionally healthy habits that help you feel good, ultimately bringing that energy to your work every day.

How can you start your day off right and set the tone for your attitude? Find things that make you feel happy or create a sense of accomplishment. Finding what works best for you will take a bit of trial and error. Experiment. Try something new each morning and note how you feel immediately afterward and in the hours that follow. After a while you will find activities that cascade positivity into your morning and, hopefully, that generates productivity throughout the day. Now, that sounds like a lot to ask from a simple morning routine, but don't worry, because it does not have to be a grand thing. Step back and identify activities that make you happy. This strategy aims to create balance by starting your day off with something joyful to encourage a productive momentum early in your day.

Take my morning routine, as an example. Currently I like to start my day off with a morning workout. After my workout (which makes me feel energized and accomplished) and before getting ready for the rest of the day, I commit ten minutes to reading a book or an article for pleasure. The demands on my time during business hours are such that I rarely have a quiet moment to read something that isn't work related. With that done, I arrive at the office feeling a small sense of accomplishment, and it helps me start off on a positive note to prepare for the daily rigors of my job responsibilities.

Be disciplined and block off time to do whatever you need to do to get in the right frame of mind. On the days when I don't follow my routine, I feel completely off. Once you create the habit, you will wonder how you survived without it.

Breaking the negative cycle

It is great to start off on the right foot, but we all know the reality of the workplace. Eventually there will be days that beat you down and take an emotional toll. Have you ever had a day where you get hammered with a series of rough emails or bad news and start to feel your frustration growing to the point where you know that your productivity is completely shot? Of course you have; you are a human in today's workforce.

The most successful people find ways to take setbacks in stride, learn from them, and persevere. On the flip side, those who fold at the first sign of distress don't stick around long enough to reap the benefit of persistence. Most people fold because they have not learned to utilize basic tools to help build the emotional fortitude required to fight on.

What happens when a series of bad things occur is that negative thoughts begin to ping-pong around in your head. If left unchecked, they will pick up momentum and dominate your thoughts. Your reality becomes distorted by blowing these issues (minor ones in many cases) into bigger problems. As these issues grow, you will likely become fixated on the negative and unable to focus on anything else. Eventually you will spiral into an unproductive state. The key to combating this is to break the vicious cycle.

Unfortunately, we all will face many setbacks in life and in our careers. The good news is that you can develop the skills necessary to grow from these setbacks. Remember, you can take valuable learning away from any situation.

When you start to feel your attitude (if not your emotional state) slipping, take a moment to reset. Resetting means slowing down the growth of negative thoughts in your head and getting back to a realistic perspective. If you don't, even things that are not negative will start to appear as issues to you. And that is not a productive mind-set to be carrying around.

Resetting can be as simple as getting away from your desk and the source of your growing frustration. A couple of other common, effective tactics are:

- Break away from your desk and take a couple of minutes to stroll in or around your office.

- Retreat to a quiet place for a few minutes to journal the negative thoughts. This can be an effective way to break the negative thought cycle.

- Do some breathing exercises. Find a quiet place free of distraction and spend several minutes taking deep, cleansing breaths with your eyes closed while picturing in your mind a peaceful scene, such as the bright blue sky or a quiet beach.

- Use different meditation practices to quiet your mind and get you back to center.

None of these approaches require a significant amount of time. Within a few minutes you can potentially break the negative cycle early and be back on a productive track. Just like starting your day off on the right foot, experiment to find what helps to bring you back to center, and keep that in your tool kit as a way of breaking the negative cycles that naturally occur in work and life.

Recognize your feelings

Sometimes we get to a place where issues have piled up (whether we failed to step away and break the cycle early or just got hit with a perfect storm of issues) to the point where we need a bigger tool to break the cycle. At this point, the emotional part of the brain is driving, and it is going a million miles an hour and navigating like an idiot (fixated on all of the negative things that can happen). If you get to this point, it can help to forcibly take the wheel from your mind's emotional side and hand it over to your logical side.

The starting point for effective management of your emotions is awareness. Begin the shift from emotional to logical by assessing what you are feeling. If something unfortunate happened, what emotions are you feeling? Are you hurt, angered, upset? When you recognize your feelings, you use different parts of your brain, initiating movement of your mental activity from the temporal lobe (emotional) to the frontal lobe (higher mental functions).

Acknowledge your feelings

Now that you are aware of your emotional state, it is time to formally acknowledge your feelings. If you are upset (and in a private place), it's okay to say out loud, "I am pissed off!" The other part of acknowledgment is to give yourself permission to feel. Acknowledge that it is perfectly normal to be upset from time to time. You are human. This acknowledgment (verbalized or written) creates additional space between emotion and logic. With the feelings clearly out there, you have taken a big step forward and are getting closer to focusing on developing a solution.

Seek out the source

By shifting to seeking out the source, you are now getting into the early stages of finding a resolution. If you are upset, find out why you are feeling this way. In most cases you already know the answer and don't need to research deeply to figure it out. In other cases, a combination of things might be in play. Either way, identify the sources and clearly outline why they have caused you to feel this way.

As an example, maybe you are upset because you were you passed up for a promotion, and the position went to someone you deemed as a less qualified internal candidate. Take the time to go deeper into what you feel. Ask yourself why getting passed up is upsetting. In this example, maybe you are envious, or harbor feelings of inferiority, or even a combination of both.

Step back and sift through your feelings. Look deeply and try to get a firm grasp on each of them. This is not a race, and don't stop the sifting at the superficial level, like I'm upset because I wanted that job. Obviously, that is the case; but what else is behind your feelings?

Once you have isolated the true sources of your feelings, it is time to shift toward an objective examination of the situation.

Learn the facts

Finally, examine the facts behind the situation that generated your feelings. As difficult as it can be at times, mindfully remove your biases from the interpretation of the facts and clearly identify the indisputable ones.

Let's revisit the passed-up-for-promotion example.

- Jenny was promoted for the internal job opportunity that you also applied and interviewed for.
- She is a couple of years younger than you.
- You don't have an overly positive impression of Jenny.

    You believe Jenny is an underperformer. How did you come to that conclusion? Upon further review, you remember that Charles, who works with Jenny, has complained about working with her. Now, question the depth of this data point. Were Charles's complaints a thorough assessment of Jenny's skills and competencies? Likely not. It could be a personality difference, or even Charles venting because he is envious. Either way, this is a flimsy stance and would not constitute an indisputable fact.

- Jenny has been in this pre-promotion position two years longer than you.
- The account she manages is the largest one in the company. It has grown since Jenny started managing it.

In this case, you may not like the decision to promote Jenny instead of you. You may have been completely qualified, but it does appear that you can make a case that the promotion of Jenny had merit. After going through this exercise, you may still feel a little slighted, but you have pulled logic into the equation and now you are in a better position to process and accept the reality.

Remember that your mind makes quick, emotionally based decisions and then rationalizes them after the fact. You need to evaluate the story you are telling yourself. Often people in these types of situations will fixate on a single emotional quality of the employee being promoted (a less seasoned employee, the luck of the draw, being on the right team, being on projects with high visibility, favoritism, etc.), and it will feel unfair and upsetting. They will rationalize their anger or envy by using the one performance data point they have, which, in this case, is Charles's complaint. Without understanding the facts surrounding his complaint, you use it as the main proof point behind your hypothesis of injustice. Exacerbating the situation, you go and vent to a friend or a trusted colleague. How do you think the colleague is going to respond when you are emotional and presenting your case with your slant? Of course they are going to agree with you. They want you to feel better, and agreeing with you is the path of least resistance.

Once you have collected all of the facts, it should be clear whether or not your feelings are valid. There will be times when you won't be right, and others when you have every reason to be upset. Either way, it is OK to have those feelings. The most important thing is how you respond to them.

Once you know, what do you do?

The last step in the process is to determine where you can go from here. This means defining the actions you are going to take to improve how you feel or improve your current situation.

> **IF YOUR GOAL IS TO GET THE PROMOTION YOU WANTED, YOU SHOULD CHANNEL THOSE FEELINGS INTO WHAT YOU CAN DO TO GET IT IN THE FUTURE, BECAUSE THAT IS ALL YOU CAN CONTROL.**

Continuing to use the promotion example, let's look at attempting to make the best of the situation. Getting angry or trying to right a wrong by stomping into the manager's office and unleashing a rambling, incoherent vent session may make you feel better in the near term, but it is not going to improve your long-term prospects. If anything, it would likely be damaging to them. Focus on what you can control. Jenny has been promoted and you cannot change that. All you can control is how you respond to this situation. If your goal is to get the promotion you wanted, you should channel those feelings into what you can do to get it in the future. Meet with the manager and share your aspirations. Ask what you need to do to achieve that next promotion. Ask if there were things you could have done differently during the vetting process that would have improved your candidacy, and then ask yourself the same questions. Turn this situation into a positive learning experience that improves your chances to get promoted by bettering yourself and making it known to your manager that you are ambitious. Constructive approaches are best.

The struggle is most people don't take the constructive approach, which ends up compounding the problem. Often, they will sit and mope or, even worse, act out. Their performance suffers and their boss begins looking at them in a less-than-positive light. The constructive framework approach is a power-ful way to bring your emotions and actions back into a productive direction. As you become more adept within this framework, whether as an influential peer or as a man-ager, you will be called upon to help work through emotionally charged situations. With this skill you can have a far-reaching impact at work, laying the foundation for being a true organizational leader.

> *An organizational leader is an individual who typ-ically provides guidance, inspiration, objectives, and operational oversight, and empowers staff to achieve the business's mission.*

HOW TO HARNESS A POSITIVE ATTITUDE

All of us start with different levels of optimism. Some people naturally have a sunny disposition, while others seem to have consistent clouds following them—and the rest of us fall somewhere in between. However, we do have the ability to improve and control this to a certain extent.

Why do you think companies participate in corporate retreats, host happy hours, or have employee appreciation activities? When executed properly, these events improve relationships and build camaraderie among the team mem-bers. Similarly, you can actively work on your attitude and strengthen it like any other skill. Optimism reconditioning is kind of like hitting the gym to strengthen your mind's ability to see the positive in situations.

The concept of learned optimism was defined by the psychologist Martin Seligman as the idea in positive psychology that a talent for joy, like any other, can be cultivated. Learning optimism is done by consciously challenging how we process information and manage our negative self-talk.

The brilliance behind this concept is that our perspectives can be reshaped. Our brains are conditioned toward confirmation bias. If we have a negative view of our workplace, we will likely find more things wrong with it (and neglect the positive elements) to confirm our stance. As we find more "evidence," we solidify and deepen the roots of our negative stance.

Confirmation bias is the tendency to find only facts that confirm one's existing beliefs or theories.

The reverse is also true. If you have a more optimistic perspective, you will be able to identify and substantiate the positive elements of your work environment.

One way to do this is to begin or close your day by jotting down three things that are positive about your work. There are no limitations. These three things could be related to your responsibilities, what your company does for its customers, the skills you are developing, and so on. Perform this exercise for a couple of weeks and you will start to see an influx of the positive elements of the job across all situations.

As a result, you bring a more positive energy to your day and the office. To further develop your optimism, shift that exercise to focus on other parts of your life as well. Finding a deeper appreciation and gratitude in all avenues of life will further perpetuate an optimistic mind-set in your career.

Also pay close attention to your self-talk. If you are being unreasonably negative to yourself, you may be unwittingly undermining your own success. Use the same positive strategy as above if you start to feel overly critical of yourself. Step back and highlight three things that you do well.

Quick tip: There are work environments that are harmful to your development and potentially to your well-being. If you are in one of these poor work environments, I'm not saying that you should attempt to will yourself into believing that it is a positive one. The purpose of the exercise is to see things as half full instead of half empty.

KEEP SCORE

We all have a competitive drive within ourselves, some more than others. This competitiveness can be channeled to enhance productivity and our overall satisfaction with our jobs, even if that competitive energy is focused on simply competing with ourselves. Businesses tap into this by using gamification as a tool.

A popular example of using gamification to engage customers is the McDonald's Monopoly game. They use it to encourage additional consumption of their products by adding a game component to their packaging (Monopoly game pieces). Ultimately, customers increase the frequency of their visits to McDonald's and find some joy in participating in the game.

In his book *Happier*, the former Harvard professor Tal Ben-Shahar describes his research that showed that employees

> *Gamification is the application of typical elements of game playing (e.g., point scoring, competition with others, rules of play) to other areas of business to encourage engagement with a product, a service, or a certain set of behaviors.*

who keep score have more fun and are more productive, even in the most repetitive jobs. He found, for example, that people who kept track of the number of boxes sorted each hour and then made a contest of it for each hour were far more productive and happy.

Now look at your job and your daily responsibilities. Think about how you can leverage this score-keeping technique to your benefit. Could you track the number of customer contacts each hour or day? Or the number of files audited and filed each hour? It may require that you get a little creative, but spend some time to think about what else you could measure and track to compete with yourself.

Try it for a couple of weeks and monitor your results. I am willing to bet you will be pleasantly surprised at the impact it has on your productivity and mood. When you are keeping score, make sure to celebrate personal bests and even reward yourself for big milestones met.

OWN IT

One of the other key elements for a strong business culture is ownership. In cultures with a high level of ownership, team members take complete responsibility for their performance and embrace the results of their efforts, regardless of the outcome.

This kind of attitude is what makes for highly productive businesses and, also, highly productive team members. Strong leaders will share the overarching plans for the organization, engage the staff for objective planning, seek regular feedback, and provide a reward system to reinforce these ownership-oriented behaviors. These activities are designed to raise the overall level of ownership within the organization. Likewise, there are things you can be doing to enhance your levels of ownership and make yourself a stronger contributor—and ultimately better positioned for that next level.

> *Owning a project or task, in a business sense, means taking responsibility for every aspect of the activity, from how it is developed and managed to the end product of the deliverable.*

Throughout this section we will look at defining characteristics that make up ownership at the employee level. Ownership is a buzzword you will hear around the workplace very often, but it is not easy to distill down into a simple form. If you were to ask a coworker to describe what ownership is, they will likely have a difficult time articulating it. However, most people are quick to recognize it when they see it in the workplace.

To own it, you must earn it

Your mind-set will play a huge role in determining your career fate. Benjamin Franklin said it best: "Diligence is the mother of good luck." If you want to get ahead in your career, you must be willing to work smarter and harder than others. If you embrace this early on, you will run laps around your competition in the office and accelerate your own personal development.

This mind-set means taking pride in going the extra mile. The difference is focusing on putting the best product out there rather than being fixated on finishing the project as quickly as possible. This is a common mistake of employees at all levels. They find themselves scrambling to complete a task or project without considering the end goal and the quality of the product delivered. They focus on completing a task on their checklist and fail to take into account how they will be viewed if their output is sloppy. Take pride in your work product and be committed to seeing a project all the way through to completion. Here are some key characteristics of employees who embody a strong ownership attitude:

- They always take ownership for their actions and work product.
- They never blame external factors for underperformance. They take full ownership for their role in the issue.
- They put in the work even when no one is watching.
- They find ways to get things done. This means not giving up at the first sign of trouble. Many people focus on why they can't get things done. Instead, these individuals are committed to completion and finding ways to persevere and achieve the end goal.

These characteristics sound simple enough, though way too many people in the business world are not willing to put in the work to take ownership. If you fully embrace the behaviors listed above, you will get noticed very quickly and establish the reputation of a strong employee.

Ownership means after-hours

There is only so much time in the day, so be prepared to work on your development outside of business hours. Schedule it and be consistent. It is easy to come home from a long day at work and plop down on your couch. Most people do exactly that. Those who want more find the discipline to complete their objectives. Figure out when and how you work best to make certain your development happens.

THOSE WHO WANT MORE FIND THE DISCIPLINE TO COMPLETE THEIR OBJECTIVES.

For example, I find it difficult to sit locked in to one task for long stretches of time. That probably speaks to my short attention span, more than anything else. As a result, I find that when structuring my time to work on a large project (like writing this book while running multiple companies), I am more productive when I block off one or two half-hour sessions each day to lock in on the task at hand. Using this approach, I pulled together my first draft of the book in five months while going through one of the most demanding work stretches in my career. Once I get rolling during one of those thirty-minute sessions, I often keep going for a longer time. Scheduling these short windows helps me get over that initial mental block or procrastination tendency.

Ownership means longer hours

Another element of the ownership mentality is expecting to put in longer hours than most of your peers—especially when you are working on a deadline. You should make sure to do everything in your power to meet all of the deadlines in front of you. I'm not saying you are required to stay late daily and work on weekends, but avoid being the person who runs for the door every night at 5:00. In every business role, there will be times when you need to go above and beyond to get the job done, and put in those extra hours to bring the project home. Ultimately, let the work dictate the time and the extra effort required.

Your manager is very aware of the hours you are keeping. If you are consistently coming late and leaving early, or are unwilling to dedicate extra time when the team is nearing a big deadline, you will appear uncommitted to the team, and it will be detrimental to your career.

A MANAGER'S VIEWPOINT

Strong managers will not be completely focused on the exact number of hours an employee is working. They should be more concerned with output and meeting deadlines. They let the work be a guide for the necessary hours in the office. There will be times when you will need to work late, but there will be times when things are quieter, and an in-tune manager will encourage you to take advantage of this slower time and get out a littler earlier.

Be conscious of the fact that this viewpoint is not a prevailing one with most managers. It is unfortunate, because they are taking a very shortsighted approach to this. Anyone can sit and fill a workday. Most strong leaders would rather have someone who cranks out a ton of work and is extremely efficient.

Long hours come with the territory if you are ambitious, but you will need to find balance and adequate time to recharge. You can't work nonstop without taking a break, because your body will break down and/or your productivity will suffer.

What an ownership mind-set isn't

Before we leave the coverage of the ownership mind-set, it is worth taking a moment to review what is not an ownership mind-set, and a couple of things to avoid. Beware if you find yourself uttering the words "That's not my job" or "I am too busy." Underneath those words is a selfish mentality. It reflects that you'd prefer to do the minimum and take little pride in the quality of your work. People with this kind of mind-set are usually quick to draw a line in the sand on where their responsibilities end and are unwilling to help or care past that career-limiting line.

If you want a funny example of cautionary tales, just search online for the annual "not my job" awards. You will find gems like this:

The picture above is worth a laugh, but it is amazing how many people do these types of things on a smaller scale and less publicly every day. Ultimately it undermines their ability to be successful.

Ownership is in everything you do

Ownership is embodied in and revealed through the quality of everything you do. At the workplace, top performers own and take responsibility for each element of their job.

Those who thrive are mindful of how they interact with others on email, at the office, and on the phone. This means proofreading every email and using a professional tone and vocabulary in all correspondence.

When completing a project, remember that it's not just about the content. How have you packaged and formatted the project? Does the formatting convey a sense of professionalism? Apple has mastered the packaging and presentation of their products. If you bought an iPhone recently, you can attest that when you open the box, it is an experience designed to reinforce the elegant high-end nature of Apple's products. You should do the same thing when packaging your work product, if it's a project or presentation. If you are not overly skilled at formatting and design, ask a friend or colleague with skills in this area to help you build a template. You want the format and packaging of your project or presentation to give the impression that you put a tremendous amount of time and energy into it. If the packaging conveys that, you will more likely than not get the benefit of the doubt when your manager or customer is reviewing your work product. You should be proud of every aspect of your output.

Put yourself out there and ask for more

To develop a reputation as someone who is eager to contribute and learn, you will need to ask for more opportunities. Know how and when to ask for more opportunities. Showing initiative sometimes requires you to go outside your job description. If something needs to get done, be willing and eager to jump on it. It demonstrates your ambition and it provides you with a learning opportunity. When you have downtime, ask your manager if there is something you can help with. Perhaps there is a project that you have been eager to participate on; if there is something that will help you develop a new skill, offer your services. Ask for permission to see if your peers could use your expertise and assistance on their current projects.

Be careful to know your limits and do not take on too much. Your can-do attitude can be exploited. People of the lazier variety could take advantage of your willingness and try to pawn off work that is clearly their responsibility.

Be mindful of your workload and do not go overboard with your initiative and overcommit. That is another recipe for disaster or burnout.

If you are completely buried, don't go around asking for projects to demonstrate your go-getter mentality, because you will be setting yourself up to fail and not complete the projects on time or at the desired quality. In your meetings with your manager, be honest about your bandwidth. If you are buried with work and your manager asks you to take on another project, make sure to accurately sum up your current position using a positive tone. For example:

> "Currently my time is consumed with projects x, y, and z. However, in __ days, I will be wrapping up projects x and y, freeing up some capacity. If this is a higher priority, I can adjust and delay the completion of projects x, y, and z by __ days. Let me know your thoughts on how to best proceed."

We will talk more about managing your brand later in the book, but this type of accountability is a key element of how you are perceived within the organization. Volunteering for projects will help you to establish a reputation internally for being ambitious and a team player.

There are people in the workforce who do the exact opposite. They will burn more time working on ways to hide from a project than they would completing it. This is lazy and doesn't make sense. You are going to be in the office anyway, so you might as well have a full day and learn something new whenever possible.

Remember, when you are assigned a project, you are being given a potential gift—an opportunity to learn, grow, and bolster your resume. Do not roll your eyes or sigh when it is assigned to you. It demonstrates a poor attitude, and that will stick with you for your tenure at the company.

Showing initiative is a very easy way to differentiate yourself. When growth opportunities or promotions are available, believe me, you will have a major leg up on your peers when you exemplify ownership on a consistent basis.

IDEAS IN ACTION

- ▶ A positive attitude is the backbone for a strong personal culture.

- ▶ Your attitude, like any other skill, can be strengthened through

  - ▷ Starting off on the right foot

  - ▷ Breaking the negative cycle

  - ▷ Optimism reconditioning

- ▶ Employees who thrive exemplify ownership through

  - ▷ Always taking ownership for their actions and work product

  - ▷ Never blaming external factors for underperformance

  - ▷ Putting in the work even when no one is watching

  - ▷ Finding ways to get things done

7

Confidence Is the
Difference-Maker

As Henry Ford put it, "Whether you think you can, or you think you can't—you're right."

Confidence is the difference-maker. When you have confidence (or pretend you do), people respond to you in ways that will significantly aid in your future success. Half (or more) of the game in sports, business, and life is belief in yourself.

BELIEVE IN YOURSELF

Confidence has a huge bearing on how you perform. It drives self-fulfilling prophecies—both positive and negative. If you believe you are going to be successful, you are, in fact, more likely to be successful. This is because:

- You are less likely to self-sabotage.
- You see the positives and opportunities in situations.
- You are more likely to get up and dust yourself off after a failure.

What are you saying about yourself with your speaking tone and the manner in which you carry yourself? Take the time to monitor them. You may be surprised at the number of ways you are undermining your success.

How are you perceived?

The way you carry yourself has a huge impact on how others view you. It is not just the words coming out of your mouth that your coworkers are evaluating; it is your tone and body language too. If you deliver your message with a lack of confidence, your coworkers will think you don't believe in your own words or—even worse—you don't know what you are talking about. Think back to a time when someone walked into the room beaming with confidence. How did that make you feel about that person?

Our minds need to categorize everything and everyone, so you most likely believed that that person was knowledgeable and competent before they even spoke a word. Think about that. Confidence is a huge advantage that gives you the benefit of the doubt, and it will take stumbling a couple of times for you to lose that status. On the flip side, if you walk in meekly, you have an uphill road to being viewed as competent.

How do you present to others?

Confidence can carry significant weight when you are presenting to others. When you present your ideas, the audience is not only listening to the words you are saying; they are evaluating how you present the material and how you carry yourself. A mentor early in my career made me aware of this phenomenon, and listening to that advice played a major role in many of my early successes. I made a conscious effort to deliver my material with conviction and confidence, and I believe it played a big part in how my ideas (and I) were embraced. Think about it this way. If someone is half-hearted in their delivery of a proposal, why should the audience care, even if the proposal has merit?

Check your tone

Take a step back and monitor your delivery when communicating with others (in both formal and informal interactions). You may find it helpful to record yourself often during different interactions and study your verbal pauses, pace, and tone. Make sure you are conveying your message in a confident and reassuring manner. A strong and confident tone comes from projecting your voice from deep in your diaphragm. Once you've practiced your delivery, record it, refine it, and adjust your voice to the proper level.

Choose your words carefully

Your choice of words contributes greatly to how people view you. Avoid using hedging phrases like *kind of, sort of,* and *maybe,* because they undermine your message and other people's perceptions of your confidence and belief in the statements you are making. Compare the two examples below and tell me which makes you feel more reassured:

- "Based on the research, I kind of think we may need to consider pursuing an alternative path."
- "Based on the research, it has become abundantly clear to me that we will need to pursue an alternative path in order to find success."

Obviously, you would feel much more confident following the second recommendation, because it is direct and definitive.

Grow your vocabulary

Another way to project confidence is to expand your vocabulary. Consult the thesaurus regularly. Learn industry terms that should be included in your vocabulary arsenal. Bolstering your vocabulary will demonstrate a strong command of the English language, which can translate into your being perceived as more competent in other areas too.

Watch the self-talk

That internal dialogue going on in your head has a way of manifesting itself into actions, behaviors, and approaches that can shape how you perform. It's important to channel and redirect it into productive directions.

Examine your internal dialogue and note the kind of conversation and tone you're engaging in.

Negative self-talk is the worst. We've all been there—when we've had negative thoughts in our head prior to a performance and then gone on to perform poorly. The self-talk was not the sole cause of the poor performance, but it was a contributing factor.

Rewrite the script in your head

The best-case scenario is to have positive and uplifting internal conversations in your head, in which your thoughts are focused on your strengths and inevitable success. But let's be realistic, that's not going to happen often for most of us. Especially right before a big event like a presentation. A healthy dose of fear and anxiety does creep in and can hijack your thoughts.

**THE BEST-CASE SCENARIO IS TO HAVE POSITIVE
AND UPLIFTING INTERNAL CONVERSATIONS IN YOUR HEAD,
IN WHICH YOUR THOUGHTS ARE FOCUSED AROUND YOUR
STRENGTHS AND INEVITABLE SUCCESS.**

When this happens, focus your internal conversation in a more productive direction. Rather than beating yourself up by focusing on your weaknesses or fears, take a practical approach to work through the situation. Let's look at someone who is waiting in the reception area of a client's office, only minutes away from delivering one of his or her most important client presentations to date, and having an internal conversation:

> *As I sit here waiting for my contact at the company, all these thoughts of doubt begin to rush in my head. What if I choke and stumble through the presentation? If I mess up in a spectacular way, I may lose my job. If that happens, how am I going to find another job . . . ?*

Stop! See how dangerous this line of thinking can be? You've likely experienced this at one time or another, where your thoughts begin to turn into a runaway train. Let's jump back into this situation and break the negative cycle.

> *Obviously, I am a little anxious and that is completely natural. This is an important meeting for me and the company. What did I do to prepare? I spent countless hours researching the client's needs, secured great pricing, and have practiced this presentation over a dozen times. I know it cold. And I have had recent success in these types of big pitches. In my last two critical presentations I have knocked them dead and won the client's business.*

Notice how the thought process changed. First, break the cycle by acknowledging your nerves, because you won't be able to push them down. Then focus your energy on any and every positive entity you can. Make sure your glass is half full. The next step is to shift your focus to practical execution. Let's jump back into this hypothetical situation again.

What am I going to need to perform my best today? When I am a little anxious, like I am today, I tend to rush my delivery. I will make sure to take my time and let my points land. Especially on my first slide—that will set the tone and pace for me throughout the rest of the presentation. Also, encourage questions during my presentation. I know this product inside and out and thrive in a question-and-answer setting. When I get to the support slide, remember to ask Bill what are the most important factors in customer support that will help them achieve their business objectives.

See how that practical shift can change the dialogue dramatically? The focus of your energy is now aimed squarely at the tactical elements that will help you perform better, rather than fixating on irrational negative thoughts.

VISUALIZE

It is commonplace for athletes at the highest levels to use visualization as part of their preparations. Studies have demonstrated the physical and psychological benefits of this practice. The power of visualization lies in demystifying the event you are concerned about. If executed correctly, your visualization will increase your confidence and comfort level going into your event, because you have already experienced the event in your mind.

Everyone's approach to visualization is a little different. Below I have outlined a common framework to start from, but feel free to tweak and modify according to what works best for you.

SET THE STAGE

Find a quiet place where you will not be interrupted. Start by taking a series of deep cleansing breaths to clear your mind.

USE ALL YOUR SENSES

This practice is most effective when you employ all of your senses so you can immerse yourself deeper into the situation, making it more realistic and impactful.

When I am preparing for a presentation, I start my practice reps by reliving what it feels like to wait right before going onstage. I am not a fan of waiting and often get a little anxious. To calm those nerves, I practice waiting to go onstage in my mind.

> *Practice reps are simulated run-throughs of a presentation or other activity where you try your best to re-create the actual environment.*

Q: What thoughts are racing through my mind?

A: The sound of the voice of the individual who is onstage before me and the song that will be playing when I walk up on the stage.

I feel the temperature of the room and the slight tension that I typically carry in my shoulders. Engaging those senses makes it feel like I am actually there waiting to go onstage.

PRACTICE

This exercise should not be completed with wishful thinking. It should be a detailed walk-through. As with any other form of practice, you gain competency by practicing whatever you are working on step by step. As you walk through each step in your mind, live and experience it like you are performing in that moment.

Visualization is a powerful preparation tactic, and if it becomes a regular part of your routine, you will see noticeable performance improvements over time.

Don't put yourself down

There are little things we do that ultimately undermine our confidence and how others perceive us. Many of us (I am guilty of this) use things like a self-deprecating sense of humor or false modesty to fit in. Don't get me wrong: There is a time and a place for these types of responses; however, they are few and far between.

Many of us will utilize false modesty or a self-deprecating sense of humor because we are not truly confident. When used regularly, it frames your message in a negative light because it plants seeds of doubt in the person receiving your message. It also can reinforce negative self-talk or insecurities that you have. For most of us, being confident is hard enough. Do not add any fuel to your "doubting" side. Instead, speak with conviction and confidence. You don't need to boast, but you need to believe in yourself and acknowledge credit for what you accomplish.

Accept compliments with grace

When someone pays you a genuine compliment, it may make you feel uncomfortable. An unconfident approach is to play it off or trivialize the compliment, saying something like, "I was lucky." Do not do that to yourself. Look the person in the eye and shake their hand while you thank them for their kind words. Let yourself enjoy the words and accept the compliment. Think about what happens after a stage performance. When the actors come out for their applause, most take a bow and soak in the recognition from the crowd. You should do the same.

WATCH WHAT YOUR BODY LANGUAGE SAYS

Posture plays a large role in how you are perceived and how you feel. Others will make snap judgments on you at first sight based on how you carry yourself. Would you rather be viewed as strong and confident or as weak and meek? Humor me for a second and participate in this little exercise, because I bet you already know more about body language than you even realize.

Close your eyes and visualize someone who is unconfident. Now jot down what you see that makes you believe they lack confidence.

What did your mental image look like? Was it someone with their chin ducked down? Maybe someone in a hunched-over or shoulders-slumped position? Or arms crossed in a protective-type pose? Avoiding eye contact? If you do a search online for images using "lack of confidence," you will see the same thing.

RESHAPING YOUR BODY LANGUAGE WILL TAKE TIME—LIKE CHANGING ANY OTHER HABIT.

Why was that exercise easy for most of us? It was easy because we see it and live it every day. The key here is to recognize what projects confidence and then be more mindful of how we carry ourselves, so we project a more confident, executive-type presence.

Reshaping your body language will take time—like changing any other habit. Take time daily to practice your posture. Be mindful and correct course when you recognize yourself slipping into older habits. Here are the key posture elements that will aid in your projection of confidence:

- Keep your chin up. Burying your chin down into your chest indicates a lack of confidence.
- Roll your shoulders back and slightly puff your chest out.
- Take up a wider stance with your feet, and rest your hands on your hips when standing. This is known as the "Superman" or "Wonder Woman" pose. Taking up larger amounts of space with your body equates to confidence.
- Make a conscious effort to make eye contact with everyone. Eye contact helps to project confidence and trust. Think back to a time when you had a conversation with someone and they never looked you in the eye. How did that make you feel about them? Likely it was a bit unsettling and you did not have an overly positive impression of them.

I have found that focusing on one area (like standing up straight) each day is easier to manage than trying to tackle all methods at once. Focus on one area for a couple of days in a row, then shift to a different focus area. This will help you build good habits in one area before shifting to another one.

Implementing these tips will help you to be perceived as more confident. Another benefit of using positive body language is it can help you feel more confident.

Throughout this section I have outlined a number of different tools you can leverage to improve your daily performance. They have been some of the most important things I've used to consistently achieve more highly productive days.

Your attitude is the underlying fuel for your performance, whether in front of others or not. The practices I've outlined are designed to replenish the confidence elements of that fuel. They certainly have propelled my career at a rate faster than I ever could have imagined.

IDEAS IN ACTION

- ▸ Tools to boost your confidence and your performance

  - ▹ Positive self-talk

  - ▹ Breaking negative thought cycles

  - ▹ Speaking with authority

  - ▹ Avoiding false modesty

  - ▹ Practice and visualization

  - ▹ Strong body language

8

Work Smarter

In today's demanding and competitive business climate, even the best companies and managers are limited in the amount of time and energy they can spend on your professional development. Even if you are fortunate and find yourself in an organization that values your development, there is still plenty you can and should do to augment the best development programs and shorten your learning curve.

The key to accelerating your personal development is to seek out opportunities to learn and grow at every turn. This means taking advantage of all the resources your organization offers you: existing education programs, your peers, and potential mentors. Additionally, your development plan can be rounded out by your activities outside the office.

> *Professional development is a training process aimed at improving one's skills and capabilities in the workplace.*

This may sound like a broken record, but *you are your own business*, so your personal development rests squarely on your shoulders. You must own every aspect of it.

In hotly contested markets, attracting top-flight talent is an arms race between companies. Businesses will go above and beyond to attract the best and brightest talent, but bringing in the talent is only part of the equation. The highest-performing organizations know that developing their talent is a vital process that ensures the quality of their people meets their current and future business priorities. When executed correctly, the development of superior talent is one of the most surefire paths to a sustained competitive advantage.

Plenty of companies do an exemplary job of this. These organizations build well-crafted plans tailored to the employee's skill development, performance management, and succession. Some examples of companies and industries known to have top talent development programs are Amazon, General Electric, Enterprise Rent-A-Car, large CPA consulting firms, and the hospitality industry.

Take Amazon: They have an intensive, month-long training and leadership program prior to hire. Similarly, Enterprise has a robust onboarding process consisting of a mix of classroom and practical field training their hires must complete before starting their day-to-day responsibilities. As employees graduate through the necessary skills for their next promotion at Enterprise, they are required to take a test and undergo a grueling interview process before they are promoted. All of this is designed to set the employee up for success as their responsibilities grow and they are faced with new challenges.

DEVELOP YOUR TALENTS IN THE OFFICE

The following points will help you start your development journey. If you execute your personalized plan with regularity and a strong focus, it can propel you to impressive heights.

The easiest, almost no-brainer approach is to take advantage of all the programs your company offers. In many cases, companies will cover the cost. I have personally benefited from company-sponsored options like high-potential groups, courses on conflict resolution and presentation skills, and tuition reimbursement. Not all of these opportunities ended up being completely relevant to my role at the time; however, I have used the skills that I developed pursuing these tangential learning opportunities throughout my career.

Once you have taken advantage of the easy-to-access training, it will take a little more effort and initiative to find the next level of opportunities to enrich your growth. They will come in the form of cross-training, cultivating relationships in the office, and securing a productive mentoring relationship.

Seek cross-training development

Cross-training is an effective way to round out your experiences and make you a more versatile and attractive contributor to your organization. It will also make you a more desirable candidate to recruiters when you apply for positions.

> *Cross-training is the practice of being trained in different roles and skills outside of your current job responsibility.*

Cross-training can occur within your current department or outside of it in a different discipline. Some organizations will have planned rotations for designated team members to switch departments and roles every few months, while others have no such formal practice.

Learning and working side by side with others outside of your department is a great way to expand your perspective on the organization as a whole. It is very easy to be constrained within your department's silo and be limited to a rather myopic viewpoint. Cross-training combats that. These types of projects will give you a glimpse into what strengths, challenges, and limitations other departments face daily. Not only will you grow as you experience new parts of the business, but you will also become more productive within your organization. Your familiarity with the inner workings of other departments will allow you to make more informed decisions and be more efficient in your work.

If there is not a formal cross-training platform in your organization, take the initiative to create your own. Ask for your manager's permission, and make sure that this activity does not get in the way of your day-to-day responsibilities. For example:

- Seek skills or responsibilities that are required for the "next level" above your current role that you do not currently possess.

  Cross-training can be a great way to learn and prepare for potential promotions. The exposure to different skills and responsibilities can give you currency with decision makers when you are evaluated for a potential promotion (it demonstrates the ability to complete tasks at the next level).

- Seek projects that require cross-departmental efforts.

  It may not make sense to request this early on in your tenure with the company and in your position. There is no set timeline on when this kind of request is appropriate. It is situational. It should take place once you have demonstrated a basic mastery of your core responsibilities, your work environment has stabilized to the point where you are able to spend a couple of hours a week away from your desk, and it will not be a major disruption to your ability to get your daily responsibilities completed.

  Cross-departmental exposure is valuable on multiple levels. You have a chance to demonstrate your talents to additional people within your organization. This showcase opportunity can pay dividends when internal openings come up in different departments. Working side by side with team members in other departments can provide valuable insights and create a more cultured view about the business as a whole.

- Ask to shadow different job functions and departments.

  Be prepared to illustrate how understanding a different job function will help your performance in your current role when you speak to your manager. If you execute your request correctly, you will likely be granted your opportunity and earn some "bonus points" with your manager for being a self-starter.

An effective cross-training platform will give you a better understanding of your organization. It also provides you with a stronger perspective of your role and its impact on your organization's objectives.

Everybody's talking: Join in

The most effective executives in the business world leverage relationships across their entire organization to get things done and make sound decisions. Much of their effectiveness can be attributed to strong relationships and a well-balanced knowledge base about the business and its inner workings.

Unfortunately, early in your career you don't have the luxury of this kind of perspective, and you don't have access to information that most executives do. But there is a way to get there—get out and start talking to people.

Workplace gossip has a justifiably poor reputation—there's nothing worse than the gossip comprising malicious rumors or speaking ill of colleagues behind their backs. There is, however, a productive kind of "gossip" that can play an important role in your workplace success, and you need to make a consistent effort to engage in it.

This type of talk comes in the form of informal conversations that can pop up in the break room, over a happy-hour drink, or at the end of a work call. They can help you learn who really pulls the strings in your organization and expand your sphere of influence beyond your department—ultimately helping you become the most connected employee at your company.

There are few employees more valuable (and overlooked) than what I call a "connector"—a person who builds relationships across departments, contributes to corporate culture, and is capable of connecting disparate, often siloed ideas into a coherent strategy. When you become a connector, even if you are early in your career and residing in the lower levels of the organization, you can provide a bird's-eye perspective on your company, and this prepares you to contribute shrewd feedback and recommendations.

As a connector, you will have access to a broader set of perspectives than most because you are engaging with other departments and understanding the business at a far deeper level (organizational strengths, weaknesses, limitations, and trade-offs that impact other departments). Additionally, your relationships become an invaluable resource that you can go to when you need to better understand something from a different vantage point. This puts you in the position to make more informed decisions and recommendations.

BECOME A CONNECTOR

You'll have to take action if you want to establish and maintain relationships and leverage the information acquired to benefit the company (and yourself) by becoming a connector.

- Schedule It

Start by blocking off two fifteen-minute windows daily to chat with team members. Swing by their desks, say hi, ask about their weekend or upcoming trip. A little small talk goes a long way. Even now at the executive level, I still block off time to make sure I am dialed in to what is going on with my team professionally and personally and make the effort to identify and assist with any potential obstacles they may face.

- Always Say Yes

If someone asks you to go for a coffee, lunch, or happy hour, try to do it (provided it doesn't impede your actual work). The amount of work information exchanged in a more relaxed environment is astounding, and you'll build deeper relationships with your colleagues.

- Establish a Broad Network

Pulling from the lessons you learned in the cross-training section, don't just socialize in your department; a well-balanced, cross-company network will provide you with a comprehensive perspective of the business as a whole. Having visibility into a broad cross section of your organization will strengthen your work and decision making, because you'll be able to see beyond your department's silo.

- Just Ask

Not sure how something in another department works? Try asking a colleague about herself and her work. Most people *enjoy* talking about themselves and what they're doing. Take a genuine interest in what your colleague is doing. You will learn something new, gain additional perspective, and become that much more valuable to your organization.

- Be a Strong Listener

Remove all distractions (devices!) and be completely present for your conversation. Digest everything that is being presented to you. Pay attention to the tone of your colleague's delivery and body language, in addition to her ideas, and to what she doesn't say. Engage in active listening. Ask relevant and clarifying questions. Restate what she says in your own words.

- Collect Feedback

Take a genuine interest in what drives success and failure within your organization. Meet with team members across your organization and collect their feedback about what made different initiatives successful or unsuccessful. Generally, people are willing to share their candid opinions on items that you are not directly related to.

Utilizing this kind of surveying technique can provide invaluable insights about what makes initiatives successful and what impediments they may face.

- Get in the Know

Ask to be included on the distribution list for regular reports—even those specific to departments outside your own. You can justify your inclusion on the list by explaining that you want to figure out ways to work across departments to benefit your job function and the performance of the company.

- Hang Out after 5:00 P.M.

Typically, leaders in an organization work later than 5:00. Staying after normal business hours can give you access to members of the leadership team and help you form relationships with them. In those later hours it is generally quieter, and those remaining have fewer demands for their time and attention. In my experience, leaders are more likely to let their guard down during the quieter after-hours because there is a sense of camaraderie with others who put in the extra time. At the very least, you will earn a few points by being perceived as more committed.

- Stay Attuned to Your Environment

It is important to know the direction of prevailing winds. What is your network saying about your business? Are people happy? Do they look stressed? Has their behavior changed recently? Is the company adding benefits (bonuses, 401(k) matches), or reducing them? Are executives communicating less with the staff? These could be indicators that things are not going as well as planned. Are they bringing in new outside talent? Are people being let go? Have you seen a recent trend of bringing in consultants? It is important to know which way your company is shifting. You never want to be blindsided by the downturn and potential loss of a job. Also, you need to know if things are going well: Those are the opportune times to ask for raises or other benefits (when appropriate).

Developing a strong network and social ties will help you become the "go-to" resource for your company—and aid you in wielding influence far greater than your title typically carries. Business, after all, is still all about people. Your ability to tap into this informal information network can be a difference-maker that takes your career to the next level.

FIND YOURSELF A MENTOR

A strong mentor/mentee relationship can be advantageous on many levels. It is important to tap into the wisdom of those who have been there and done that. A great way to shortcut your learning curve is to leverage the years of knowledge obtained by others. Because of their many years of experience or their invaluable perspective, mentors play a critical role in your career advancement. Developing a strong network of mentors is an extremely powerful tool to add to your business's arsenal.

Your objective for developing a network of mentors is to find a group of individuals that you can trust and meet with on a semiregular basis (quarterly or at least a couple of times a year). Make sure to pull together a group that has a wide variety of experiences and skills.

For me, having a group of mentors with a wide variety of experiences has been extremely valuable. Just as a connector extracts value from a wide range of connections within an organization, a diverse group of mentors has helped me by providing different perspectives and expertise throughout my career. My mentors are a group of trusted advisors that I call my personal board of directors for my "business." I have been fortunate enough to tap into their experience to prepare and watch out for common missteps when I've encountered a new work experience. Without their guidance, I would have likely made some of those common mistakes and stumbled through those new-to-me situations.

I am grateful to these individuals who have been so generous with their time and wisdom. I can honestly say that I would not be where I am today without them.

Who mentors best?

There will be times in your relationship that your mentor will need to tell you that you don't have your head on straight. You want to make sure that your mentor is not afraid to be honest and critical when necessary.

A good mentor is someone with more experience in a specific area of business or life than you currently possess. They have a level of professional or personal success that you are striving for. They should also be a good person, someone you can trust and confide in. You should feel safe sharing and being vulnerable with this person, because you need to get to the core of issues, without having to worry about offending anyone or overstepping your bounds. It is also important that they:

- Are willing to spend time with you on a regular basis
- Are willing to be very honest with you
- Understand the mentor/mentee relationship and process

Solid mentors will be hard to find, so don't be discouraged if it takes time to establish quality mentor/mentee relationships. Given the scarcity of quality mentors, make sure to do everything in your power to maintain the relationship.

Getting and keeping your mentor

You are probably wondering how to get a busy person to take time out of their schedule to help you. It simply starts with asking your potential mentor if they would be interested in being your mentor.

How you approach your prospective mentor will depend on your current relationship. If it is an individual with whom you have a strong relationship and converse with on a regular basis, then it can be as easy as simply approaching the individual directly and stating that you admire a certain quality they possess, and you believe you could learn a great deal from them. Ask them if they would mind if you took them out for coffee or lunch and picked their brain once a quarter. If you do not have a preexisting or strong relationship with your prospective mentor, then you will need to take a more formal approach. A good way to do this without putting the person on the spot is to write an email asking if they would be willing to mentor you. The elements of this email will include sharing your career background and experiences, what your career objectives are, a little flattery highlighting the experience or traits you admire about them, and what you would like to accomplish from a mentoring relationship with them.

If they accept, make sure to be very organized for your mentoring sessions. This means preparing your questions and sending them over to the mentor in advance. They are sharing their knowledge with you, and in exchange for that you must be respectful of their time. Don't forget to express gratitude. The money you spend on coffee or lunch will be one of the best financial investments you can make.

Don't take your mentor for granted

As the person receiving the mentoring, the burden of responsibility to keep the relationship going rests with you. Like any other relationship, it takes cultivation and care. Make sure to call your mentor on a consistent basis (every other month or so). Share some of the wins you've experienced in your career. Make a special point to acknowledge how their feedback played a role in your victories. Ask them about how they are doing personally and professionally. Try to find things you could do to help them so the benefits are not just flowing one way. This is a two-way street; they need to feel like it is a mutually beneficial relationship.

Some of my mentors have been with me for over a decade. They have helped with new job opportunities, turning around businesses, assessing problems personal and professional, and I have even had the pleasure of providing guidance to some of them as my experience has grown. When managed correctly, the mentor/mentee relationship is an extremely rewarding experience that will help to drive your professional effectiveness.

I can attest to this firsthand. One of my early mentors helped me through my first big public presentation. I was completely in my own head and was a mess. My mentor, Steve, gave me a framework for how to prepare and a couple of tactics to manage my stage fright. Now, it was not the greatest speech, but it was solid enough to get the job done and ultimately laid the framework for me to become a skilled public speaker.

DEVELOP YOURSELF OUTSIDE THE OFFICE

You can make great strides in your professional life in the office by leveraging what your company provides and tapping into the knowledge and experience of your mentors. The single biggest contributor to my climb through the career ranks was my commitment to professional improvement outside of the four walls of my office.

Your mind is a muscle capable of expansive growth, and many people take this for granted. Your brain needs to be trained regularly to maintain sharpness and continual progress. Wisdom takes time to obtain. However, those who put in the extra time and out-work their peers can accelerate their learning process significantly.

> **THE SINGLE BIGGEST CONTRIBUTOR TO MY CLIMB THROUGH THE CAREER RANKS WAS MY COMMITMENT TO PROFESSIONAL IMPROVEMENT OUTSIDE OF THE FOUR WALLS OF MY OFFICE.**

Cliff Young is a perfect example of how to out-work others with a consistent and focused effort. A sixty-one-year-old Australian potato farmer turned marathoner, Young won a 543.7-mile endurance race from Sydney to Melbourne, beating world-class racers who were less than half his age and were backed by large sponsors like Nike. This race is considered among the world's most grueling ultramarathons. So how did Young, this newcomer to racing, beat his younger and far more experienced competitors? He outworked them. He ran at a slow pace and trailed the leaders for most of the first day, but he kept running while the others slept, taking the lead the first night and maintaining it for the remainder of the race. His secret was that he slept far less than the other racers and eventually won the entire race by ten hours.

This is the way to view your training opportunities outside of the office. If you put in a little work (say, fifteen to thirty minutes) most evenings, you can gain ground and even surpass your "competitors" while they are idle.

The rest of this chapter shows different ways to stay sharp and grow your mental capacities outside the office.

Be curious

The easiest way to consistently grow your knowledge base is to be curious. Take an interest in how things work. When you meet people and they tell you what they do, ask them about their job and industry. Learn about what it takes to be successful in that role, what challenges they encounter, or how the economy impacts them. When watching TV, mix in a documentary or a behind-the-scenes story about different businesses.

Taking a general interest in how things work can expose you to many new worlds. I am consistently surprised by how often a person I met at a party, conference, or event has helped me down the road—either through my newfound understanding of a new business segment or as an individual who possesses expertise in an area that can help me with a future challenge.

Always be on the lookout for opportunities to learn how things work. With this mind-set in place, you will become a lifelong learner and knowledgeable person—or at the very least, you will be an interesting person to have a conversation with!

Get smart

Early in your career, it can be somewhat intimidating to develop fluency in what is going on in the business world in general. Like learning a new language, immersion training is the most effective way to develop your fluency.

What can initially seem daunting can become quite easy when you know where to find information. The key is to tap into a multitude of sources (books, websites, business channels, magazines) on a regular basis. Don't worry about aiming for fluency right away; just engage with these outlets consistently to stay sharp and current on what is going on in the business world.

Read, read, read

Business books are a great place to start improving your business IQ. Dedicate time to read regularly. Even if you are buried by commitments, chip away at the reading. I block off at least ten minutes a day. This time is sacred, no matter what I am reading. Get creative! If you have a long commute, get audiobooks or listen to podcasts.

Try to have the books you are reading connect to your development plan. Mix in topics that are new to you or are your weak spots, but don't forget to read up on areas where you are strong. Try to read multiple books on each topic, for a more well-rounded perspective. If you are short on time, find official summaries of books online. They provide a quick way to learn the high points of a book you might want to read later.

Once you finish reading a book, make your own short book report. The whole point of reading is to take away something from the book. As I'm reading, I highlight text that I find valuable and earmark pages. Once I complete the book, I go back through each of these pages and create a "key takeaways" report. These reports don't need to be overly deep. A simple list of bullets will suffice. This way you can reference all this information very quickly and implement its use in everyday life. That's the whole point of reading, right?

MY TOP BOOK RECOMMENDATIONS

These favorites are full of great and practical advice on how to improve.

- *The 7 Habits of Highly Effective People* by Stephen R. Covey

- *Good to Great* by Jim Collins

- *MIndset: The New Psychology of Success* by Carol S. Dweck

- *Execution: The Discipline of Getting Things Done* by Larry Bossidy and Ram Charan

- *Failing Forward* by John C. Maxwell

- *What Every Body Is Saying* by Joe Navarro

- *Crucial Conversations* by Kerry Patterson, Joseph Grenny, Ron McMillan, and Al Switzler

- *Influence: The Psychology of Persuasion* by Robert B. Cialdini

- *Switch: How to Change Things When Change Is Hard* by Chip and Dan Heath

- *Wooden: A Lifetime of Observations and Reflections On and Off the Court* by John Wooden with Steve Jamison

Subscribe to a couple of business magazines too. They are good resources for deeper dives into relevant topics.

Allot some time every day to scan the business pages, read *The Wall Street Journal,* or visit CNN Money, CNBC, *The Economist, Business Insider,* Google News, or any source to get a quick scoop on what is happening in the business world today. Even a quick five-minute scan can provide a snapshot of the day's events. These are great sources for general business knowledge and awareness of major trends. If you are looking to go deeper into a specific specialty or discipline, an online search will help you find publications and websites dedicated to your given area of interest.

Cable news networks can be fruitful resources for current events and business happenings. If you are working out at the gym on a cardio machine, put on CNBC or Fox Business. You can be distracted from the heart-racing workout and pick up some informational nuggets.

When you first start to visit these outlets for business information, it may not make sense to you what is going on. Don't be deterred. Stick with a diet of healthy consumption, and you will start to pick things up more quickly.

All brains need exercise

Use it or lose it. Find ways to keep your mind active and engaged. It is easy to turn off your mind when you leave the office, but this muscle needs and craves additional stimuli. A regular dose of simple activities can help you to stay sharp and keep your mind ready for the challenges ahead.

Cognitive training is a relatively new area and is evolving quickly. Several brain-training websites claim and aim to help you think better and faster. The early research is relatively mixed, but many of us have realized the benefits of regular mental engagement. The science is still new here.

Lumosity's platform is based on neuroplasticity. Neuroplasticity is the relatively recent discovery that the brain, much like a muscle, can change shape and adapt to the challenges it is faced with. In other words, if you use a particular part of your brain enough on a particular skill, that part of the brain will grow larger and you will get better at that skill.

Another common benefit cited for regular engagement is delaying the effects of aging on your brain. I recommend visiting and trying for yourself some of the services offered at sites like Lumosity and NeuroNation.

Puzzles, crosswords, and other mind games are another way to keep your edge and make sure your analytic skills stay sharp.

Learning new skills engages your brain and strengthens its connections. Try to find new hobbies, learn a new language, or attempt to get proficient at a basic task with the opposite hand. Not only will your mind benefit, but you may also find another stress-relieving hobby for your free time.

Passive activities like watching TV can be healthy escapes in today's hectic world—when enjoyed in small doses. This kind of escape is good in moderation, but too much can be mind-numbing. The increasing popularity of streaming services and on-demand entertainment makes it far easier to binge and waste significant chunks of time. Make sure you do your best to avoid getting into a rut of overuse that could ultimately stunt your cognitive and creative development.

Remember to follow Cliff Young's lead when it comes to your training. This is a long race, so you don't have to attack this area at a breakneck pace. Just be consistent and dedicated and you will come out ahead.

STAYING ON TOP

If you have made it this far in the book, the prospect of implementing preparation techniques, tips, and practices can seem a little bit overwhelming. And you're right. Implementing even a handful of these practices and ambitiously following your career dreams takes a great amount of work and energy. That is why it is important to find time to rest so you can attack the next day.

When we are young, our minds and bodies are resilient and able to bounce back almost effortlessly. This youthful resiliency allows us to survive late nights, poor eating habits, and demanding schedules. It doesn't last long, and even with that youthful resiliency you are not putting yourself in the best position to thrive if you have poor habits. As you leave your twenties it becomes even more important to use proper maintenance to thrive and survive a demanding schedule. Here are a few guidelines to help you operate at optimal capacity.

Take a break

Give your mind and emotions a break several times throughout the day. Mark it on your calendar so you don't allow your busy schedule to steal these necessary breaks. Discover the break activities that you find most therapeutic.

- Take a five-minute walk around the building.
- Chat with a friend.
- Read something non-work-related.

Personally, I crave physical exertion, so I typically gravitate toward moving activities for my breaks, one in the morning and two in the afternoon. When working extremely long hours, I find it necessary to fit in a mid-afternoon workout to help me reset and power through a late night of work. Ultimately you will need to find the activities that work best for you. Just make sure that whatever you do, it complies with your organization's and manager's policies regarding breaks.

Shut down and take off

One of the most effective ways to avoid feeling drained is to fully use your time off. This means at the end of the day you should avoid constantly checking your email for messages that come in after hours (which I am often guilty of). Being connected is a double-edged sword. The accessibility is great for productivity in the short run; however, it is draining over time to those individuals who are always on.

As long as there are no emergency situations or tight deadlines looming, a solid practice is to establish a set time for you to be completely "dark" from email and work calls.

Shut down your laptop and phone email by 7:00 p.m. every day. On weekends, allow yourself to check your email only once—on Sunday morning. This is a solid practice to utilize at all levels. It provides uninterrupted work and think time. If yours is a customer-facing role, you will need to be "live" during the required windows. But most companies will build in admin windows for service and sales people who fall into these categories.

Along the same lines, take your vacations. Ever since the last economic downturn, people have been more afraid to take time off. And when time is taken, we are checking email every single day, trying to prove that we still add value to the organization. This comes from a deep-seated fear that the company may realize it can continue without you. Try to remember that you are a talented, significant asset. Put the laptop down and recharge yourself.

Use your weekends, evenings, and vacation time to recharge. When you are out of the office (unless it is an emergency), leave the office behind. You need to relax just as hard as you work. Find activities that help you replenish so that you can attack the next business day or week.

Make sure to take a lunch. Your body and mind need to take a break in the middle of the day. You will be more productive when you return.

Remember that your mind is a muscle that you can build up, but like all muscles, it needs a resting period to assist with the recovery process. If you don't provide that, it will falter, just like any overused muscle.

Fitness and food

Physical fitness is an important part of maintaining your health and gives you the energy to power through the workday. You do not need to be the fittest person on the planet; but a consistent workout schedule where you get your heart rate up will provide you with more energy and expand your mental capacities. There are countless studies touting the positive impact exercise has on your mind.

Also start being mindful of your diet. Food is your fuel, and if you put poor fuel in, you are not going to get the output you desire. You don't have to go overboard, but try to improve your diet. In my twenties, my diet was brutal. I noticed as my work demands grew in my late twenties and into my thirties, I started to feel more sluggish. I started choosing healthier snacks instead of my staples—chips and cookies. I substituted grapes, a variety of vegetables with hummus dip, and raw, unsalted nuts into my diet. On top of that, I started eating several healthy dinners a week. It made a big difference in how I felt and my ability to produce in my daily work.

Sleep

Consistent, quality sleep has been proven to help you perform your best and live longer. This should be reason enough to take sleep seriously, but many of us are guilty of not giving sleep its due. We mask the effects of lack of sleep through caffeine and energy drinks.

Everyone is different. Some people will perform optimally after six hours of sleep, and others may need eight hours to get there. Track your sleep. Identify the times when you wake up energized and can perform your best. How much sleep did you get? If you want to go deeper into your sleep analysis, there are free and paid apps that you can use.

For those who struggle to fall asleep, develop a consistent routine for sleeping. Aim to fall asleep around the same time every night. Create an environment conducive for sleep. That means a dark, quiet, and cool place. Avoid screen time right before bed. Research has demonstrated that lighting from screens (like laptops, tablets, and phones) disrupts your ability to sleep. Instead, try reading a book for ten or fifteen minutes to unwind.

On weekends, or outside the constraints of a nine-to-five job, naps are a great way to reenergize. Naps can lift productivity and mood, lower stress, and improve memory and learning. For optimal results, naps should be short in duration. An ideal target is between twenty and thirty minutes.

If you are ambitious and intend to implement many of the development tools and practices outlined throughout this chapter and the book, you will place great demands on your mental, emotional, and physical energy regularly. You will need to put yourself in the best position from a rest and replenishment standpoint, in order to continue to pack more progress into each of your days than most people. Use your time off wisely, and create healthy habits to ensure your success.

IDEAS IN ACTION

- ▸ Take full advantage of all the development opportunities available to you in the office.

  - ▹ Use the formal training platforms and tuition reimbursements offered by your company.

  - ▹ Seek ways to engage with other departments (cross-train).

  - ▹ Build relationships so you can be in the know and create a strong network of internal advocates.

  - ▹ Tap into the wisdom of those who are more experienced than you, with a mentor.

- ▸ Pursue regular personal development outside of the office.

  - ▹ Exercise your mind regularly to keep your brain engaged and sharp.

  - ▹ Proactively seek out content to stay up-to-date on industry and business trends that can impact your company.

- ▸ If you are ambitious, be prepared to take good care of yourself to keep pace with the extra demands your training will put on your mind and body.

  - ▹ Practice solid habits like eating healthy and getting plenty of sleep.

MANAGING YOUR PERSONAL BRAND

If your managers and coworkers (your "customers") love your brand, they are more likely to provide you with opportunities to grow and to work on higher-visibility projects—ultimately giving you the opportunity to advance in the company and beyond.

Brand management is the analysis, planning, and execution of how a brand engages with its customers and target market, and how they perceive the brand. Key elements of brand management are the product itself, its cost, its design, its packaging, its in-store presentation, and, ultimately, customer satisfaction. A strong relationship with its target market is essential for the success of any business. Successful organizations invest significant amounts of resources to maintain, improve, and uphold the brand in high esteem. Since customers are more likely to buy from a brand they love, proper and successful brand management results in higher sales.

The same is true for your career.

A secret to the success of your personal brand management is to make your brand into an aspirational one. Aspirational brands like Rolex, BMW, and Mercedes appeal to a broad audience. But only a limited portion of this audience can afford these brands, due to their limited availability and high price tags. These brands are powerful precisely because consumers crave them and will work to attain them.

> *Aspirational brands are those that a large percentage of the population would like to own but only a limited group can afford. This exclusivity, due to limited supply, enhances their desirability and demand.*

As the Business of You, you should model yourself after these types of brands. Think in terms of making yourself into a rare talent and crave-worthy employee for your customer base, which is comprised of:

- Primary customer—your manager(s)
- Potential customers—other departmental managers, leaders of the organization, customers, vendor partners, and managers in competitive businesses
- Brand zealots singing your praise—coworkers, peers, customers, and vendor partners

While creating your brand, it is important to craft and promote yourself correctly. To manage your brand well, you will need to create professional polish, market your product through strong communication skills, and harvest strong relationships with your customers by mastering interpersonal business skills. If you do it right, your business can be one of the brands that employers will seek.

9

Developing Professional Polish:
The Packaging Matters

Billions of dollars each year are spent on research and design elements for product packaging. While packaging may not be the sole reason customers decide to purchase an item, it is a powerful factor in the decision-making process. Ultimately, it can make or break the purchasing decision. Customers will factor in how the packaging looks and makes them feel. It can capture their attention and even generate an impulse buy. Additionally, post-purchase, the packaging can reinforce strong feelings about the product and company.

When evaluating the level of quality for packaging, you will notice several key attributes. Strong packaging stands out and captures attention, has a distinct brand mark that makes it easy to identify, and triggers an emotional response. These are the same attributes you should strive for when establishing your packaging or professional polish.

As highlighted earlier, Apple's packaging for an iPhone or a MacBook is an intentional experience designed to make you feel special as you open your new device, and it reinforces the characteristic sleekness and elegance of the brand. Toys and food are other segments that spend healthy amounts in this area. Their focus is about capturing attention to get you to make a buying decision, while Apple's focus is about reinforcing certain feelings about your purchase and the brand.

DEFINE YOUR PERSONAL BRAND

Take a moment to think about what your work and professional packaging say about your brand today. What do your presence, presentation skills, attitude, and work product say to your customers? Are your best attributes in the fore-front? You want your personal brand to convey your strongest characteristics, the ones most likely to advance your career.

Identify your strongest attributes

Think about your strongest attributes to demonstrate to those who can influence your career. These attributes should be true to your core identity. In general, leaders of organizations value certain traits.

COMMON ATTRIBUTES OF HIGHLY VALUED TEAM MEMBERS

- Reliability

The person will get the work done correctly and in a timely manner.

- Trustworthiness

The person will work hard and do the right things, even when no one is watching.

- Competence

The person possesses the technical skills to effectively manage responsibilities.

• Ownership

The person sees things through and owns the outcome of the project and task.

• Ability to be a team player

The person is willing to volunteer to do whatever is necessary for the greater good of the team and the organization.

• Resourcefulness

The person finds ways to learn or obtain the necessary information to accomplish the objective without previous experience or requiring much additional support.

The key to harnessing these attributes and any others you want to convey is to be consistent and embody them in everything you do in and around the office, so that your brand will become identifiable. As you work through the rest of this chapter, take note of your targeted characteristics, and find ways to weave them into your own package—your professional polish. As an example, if one of your key brand characteristics is creativity, find ways to highlight that attribute. Taking a different approach to presentations or layouts for projects can be a simple but effective way for you to emphasize your creative skills.

STAND OUT IN A POSITIVE WAY

Your personal packaging should stand out from others in a positive way. It should convey the message that you are a professional and competent with your own personal flair.

A cornerstone to career advancement and professional success is projecting a professional presence consistently. Every moment of your life you are being evaluated by the way you speak, the words you use, how you look, your non-verbal communication, your presence, and etiquette. In the workplace, these evaluations determine whether you get the big project, more responsibility, or even that next promotion. That is why it is essential that you manage all the elements under your control to project your best you. This section outlines the framework for cultivating your best professional presence through looking the part and acting the part.

Appearance—walk the walk

Professional appearance comes down to the basics of how you dress and groom yourself. Your company's policy should provide solid guidance on what is appropriate for your workplace. Take note of what your manager wears to work as a guide to what is appropriate. In many cases, a manager will dress a notch or two above what the policy dictates. A safe practice is not to flirt with the lower limits of what is deemed acceptable in the office. "Dress for the position you want" is an adage that still rings true. Whenever there is a question, err on the side of overdressing rather than underdressing.

> **"DRESS FOR THE POSITION YOU WANT" IS**
> **AN ADAGE THAT STILL RINGS TRUE.**

Even on casual Fridays, or if you work in a very casual environment, present yourself positively. Casual days and casual work environments are not an excuse to dress like a slob. Look put-together, because it will reflect positively on you. You can be casual but still look professional. And even in the most casual environments, there will be times where you will need to dress up for customers.

The grooming guidelines listed here may seem obvious, but it's surprising how many people in the workplace don't even follow these basics.

- Hair should be well maintained. Get it trimmed regularly. Facial hair should be treated the same way (beard, mustache, eyebrows, nose, ear).
- Nails should be trimmed and kept short. They should be clean.
- Brush your teeth, floss, and use mouthwash. Regularly visit the dentist. Bad breath can be a career killer.
- Good hygiene is expected of you. Bathe regularly and use deodorant. Don't overdo it with the perfume or cologne.

Be mindful of how you carry yourself and how you will be perceived. If you use strong posture and positive body language cues consistently, you can help to reinforce the professional polish you are hoping to convey to your customers. Remember the basics of positive body language: Head up and shoulders back is confidence personified. Regularly monitor your body language to ensure you are developing a consistent habit of carrying yourself in a positive manner.

Talk the talk

The way you speak can be quite telling. Your elocution needs to be consistent with your professional brand. Your tone, pace, word selection, and how fluidly you verbalize your thoughts cause those around you to judge your intelligence, technical aptitude, character, and ethics. Step back and take a good look at all the elements of your speech patterns. Are you broadcasting the kind of signals to your customers that you want to? Let's assess where some opportunities for improvement may reside.

Start by recording a few of your common conversations. These days, almost every phone has a recording device. Listen to those conversations and take note of your tendencies:

- Was there a common verbal pause (um, you know, frankly, right, so) you used?
- Were the pace and tone of your speech appropriate for the purpose of your conversation?

- Did you use slang or more casual terms (like, totes, dude) that would give off a less-than-professional tone?
- Ask yourself how you could have been more effective at communicating your message.

After conducting the recording-and-reviewing exercise a few times, you should be able to pick out a few speech tendencies that you can improve. Plan to focus on one item at a time. For example, try to catch yourself using an element of your verbal pauses (like the use of "um") in every conversation you have for the next week, and stop using it. During this week you'll become very aware of the words that come out of your mouth during conversation. It will take practice, but if you focus on it, you will start to notice every time you are about to use an "um," and then stop saying it.

Pay close attention to these verbal pauses. When overused, you come across as less credible, and people will focus on how often you use your verbal pauses rather than your content. Removing them will help you sound more polished.

Once you have mastered this, move on to the next tendency you are working on. With a little practice, you can break yourself of these undermining habits.

Cursing and other offensive language is not appropriate in the workplace. It reflects poorly on you and your judgment. Same goes for offensive topics.

If you use slang, you will likely come across as immature—probably not what you want to have associated with your brand. Graduate from the slang to portray your professional self in the workplace.

Don't try to use big words if you don't fully grasp their definitions. Speak plainly. Be an effective communicator by delivering the message clearly and concisely. Your end goal is to convey information. The incorrect use of words can make it much more difficult to decipher the ultimate message.

Another common mistake is to be out of sync with the other person in your conversation, or your audience. This can happen when we let emotions dictate our delivery. As an example, a team member comes to you with a sensitive topic that makes you a little uncomfortable. The teammate is delivering the message in a slow and nervous manner. Instead of rushing through the dialogue because of your uneasiness, take the time to adjust your pace and deliver your responses in a calm and soothing manner.

Successful business-development professionals try to mirror the pace of others when they are conversing with them. In one-on-one communication, it can be powerful to mirror the pace and tone of those with whom you are engaging. It can help to put the audience at ease and is an impactful way to help you relate with them.

Finally, hedging phrases (kind of, likely, I believe so) are credibility-killers, and they ultimately undermine beliefs others may have of your thoughts and you. When you are definitive, speak with conviction. Don't hedge.

Try your best to minimize these potential pitfalls and follow these basics to help to create a professional package that will positively reinforce your skills and talents for your customers. The key is to be consistent with the brand you are trying to convey. Make sure your words, presence, and appearance reinforce that brand.

Google is a good example. The brand is about efficiency and organizing the world's data. Go to the homepage, which you'll see is clean and free of clutter and unnecessary text and links. Google may use playful imagery to highlight some quirky elements of the brand, but the homepage is all business.

And the award goes to . . .

Have you ever wondered why businesses are quick to flaunt awards and recognitions on their packaging, marketing, and advertising materials? These recognitions or endorsements serve as a credibility badge. If you don't know anything about a business, you are more likely to quickly assume that it is reputable when it trades on the value of the award and the organization that provided it. This third-party validation creates a halo effect that positively associates the brand with the other business. You should be using the same strategy when developing your personal brand. In your career, you can leverage a handful of credibility badges to enhance how you are viewed throughout your organization.

PROFESSIONAL CERTIFICATIONS

One powerful credibility badge is professional certification. Research what personal certifications are available in your role or industry. These certifications are a tangible representation of knowledge and expertise in your role. As an example, if you are a project manager, the PMP (Project Management Professional) certification is one of the most important and prominent certifications for its industry. It is a tangible demonstration of skills and experience that can elevate how you are viewed. Additionally, these types of certifications help you command a higher salary than those without certifications could expect.

EDUCATION

Degrees are a great way to round out your knowledge base and develop new skills. Your degree and the institution where you received it are badges that can be marketed to the benefit of your brand. Why do you think you will see JD or MBA, for example, at the end of a person's name? This is a tangible way to demonstrate your knowledge and accomplishments.

PROFESSIONAL ORGANIZATIONS

Are there any professional organizations in your industry? As an example, in the franchising industry the International Franchise Association is the biggest and most reputable in the space. Being a member carries some clout with others in the franchising field. Additionally, this organization has its own certifications and designations to enhance your involvement and knowledge (real and perceived) in the industry.

Professional organizations can be powerful validators of your commitment and knowledge of the industry. They can serve as part of your personal badge. Therefore, it is worthwhile to research what organizations exist in your industry.

ONLINE FOOTPRINT

One of the first things potential employers or bosses do is research candidates on the Internet. Make sure your online footprint conveys professionalism. This means a professional headshot on LinkedIn and a well-organized, well-crafted outline of your accomplishments and skills. Also, look at your social media presence. If a potential employer were to stumble across your profile on Facebook or Instagram, what would they think? There is nothing wrong with having a good time; however, if your social media postings are littered with pictures that convey a less-than-professional image, your current and potential customers may get the wrong impression.

THE COMPANY YOU KEEP

Even though it may seem superficial, people will be judging you based on the company you keep. Do you spend most of your time with people in your organization who are notorious for having a bad attitude? Be careful, because it is easy for decision makers in your organization to lump you into a group with them, ultimately harming your career prospects. It's not that you must end friendships, but understand that the group of people you spend time with in the office will reflect upon you, good or bad. That is why it pays to have a wide-ranging friendship network within your company to convey positive aspects about your brand—that you're relatable, or well connected.

As you can see, there are a lot of badges you can leverage to reinforce a positive image of your personal brand. Be on the lookout for other badges that provide a tangible quantification of your abilities. Achievements like awards, or being quoted in a publication, can go a long way in lending you and your brand additional credibility.

Acting the part

Your aspirations should dictate how you go about acting the part of a professional. Because the majority of your coworkers won't see you in action working,

a big part of the opinion they will form of you will revolve around your perceived competence, how you carry yourself around the office, and how you
handle interpersonal interactions. It is important to follow proper social and
professional etiquette to help shape your coworkers' perceptions. These basic
behaviors are fundamental to exuding professional polish in your workplace.

PUNCTUALITY AND USING YOUR TIME

Get to work and scheduled meetings on time. *On time* means at least a few
minutes early. Your coworkers and managers will notice if you are consistently
late or sneaking out early. Lack of punctuality shows that you don't respect
others, you don't respect the rules of the office, and you aren't fully invested in
the organization. People will notice you in a positive way if you are consistently
on time. It conveys your command of your day and workload that others will
respect. This is a surprisingly simple way to impress others.

Along the same lines, be aware of the optics associated with how you manage your time. You don't want to be known as the person who consistently is
the first one out of the office the moment the clock hits 5:00 p.m. It sends off
signals that you are counting down the seconds until work is done. Even if that
is true, don't do it. (If that is the case, then start looking for another job that
you can enjoy.)

Additionally, don't waste time. It is very easy to get a negative reputation in
the office if every time someone is looking for you, you're on the phone, actively
texting, playing on social media, or walking around socializing. If you have a lot
of free time, ask your manager if there are any projects that you can assist with.
Next, look at what you can do from a professional development perspective. Be
mindful of your use of time and habits in the office and what that demonstrates
to others in the workplace evaluating you.

QUALITY WORK

Managing your work like a pro is the most direct way to demonstrate professional polish and embody the marketing elements that you want to convey to

your customers. A foundational element of your professional packaging is to meet and beat your deadlines with quality. Be organized behind the scenes to ensure completion of your tasks, and avoid having to rely on others for reminders of project deadlines.

When it comes to your work product, don't do the bare minimum. Be thorough. Evaluate the task at hand from many different angles and challenge yourself and your team to produce the best possible product.

GOING ABOVE AND BEYOND

Say you're supposed to do a competitive analysis for your supervisor. The bare-minimum analysis would consist of a quick read through the websites of the competitive companies and a surface-level analysis. If your supervisor asked you to stick to the bare minimum, fine. But if not, and you want to stand out, think about ways to go beyond expectations. Are there any competitive analysis frameworks out there you should be modeling your work from? Do online research on potential frameworks, examples, or similar projects for inspiration before jumping into your actual research. Then dig deeper, like reviewing what kind of industry trade magazines and websites you can assess. How about customer research that has been conducted on this segment? Could you conduct some firsthand user or customer research?

See the difference? With this approach, you're looking for ways to enhance your work product. This is what it means to own the outcome, rather than simply checking the box and doing the bare minimum of what was asked. Find ways to consistently overdeliver for all your projects, and your customers will become raving fans who see great potential in you.

> *Internal resources are assets that your company possesses that you can use to help with projects and other deliverables. Resources can be coworkers with skills, or an internal library of past projects, research, reports, or industry-specific data.*

When tackling a project, don't forget to use every resource at your disposal, like your strong network of internal resources. As outlined in "Everybody's Talking" from chapter 8, establish relationships throughout the organization. These relationships can help you with potential requirements that are outside your area of expertise and give you new information.

MANAGING A PROJECT

In almost every role, you will find yourself in the position of managing a project. It could be a major project involving multiple departments or a smaller project consisting of your efforts and some research. Given the regularity of project management in everyday business responsibilities, it is important to understand a foundational approach to ensure that you are prepared to succeed and project a level of professionalism when called upon to manage a project.

Handling a customer complaint is a common project responsibility for people early in their careers. If charged with this project, you are responsible for resolving the customer's issue and effectively communicating with the customer throughout the resolution process. In some cases, you would need to work with other departments to completely resolve the issue or, in other words, complete the project.

> **MANAGING A PROJECT IS A GREAT GROWING EXPERIENCE THAT WILL STRETCH YOU AND REQUIRE A WIDE MIX OF SKILLS.**

Regardless of the project's size, if you are the lead on the project, remind yourself that you are completely responsible for the product delivered. That means you need to own every aspect of the project. The end product is how you will be evaluated. See the project through to the end. That does not mean you must complete 100 percent of the work (though in some cases it may), but it does mean that you need to closely manage the work product and the timelines for all activities surrounding the project. Managing a project is a great growing experience that will stretch you and require a wide mix of skills. You will often need to shift between roles (cheerleader, therapist, mediator, decision maker, accountability buddy, problem solver, and so on). This wide range of demands will help you develop a broader set of skills.

Let's discuss a few methods to increase your effectiveness and avoid common mistakes when managing a project.

When working with others, you will need to use some skills to motivate and persuade the project team. Often you will be getting help from other departments and even from staff members who could outrank you in the corporate hierarchy, and your project may not be a high priority for them. That is why it is important to utilize the following practices to motivate and drive the project team forward toward successful completion.

- First, clearly identify the objective of the project and how it fits into the broader objectives of the organization. This will help connect the participants to the purpose of the project. Make sure they know they're doing the work for the benefit of the project itself, and not because you're asking it of them. This is an important distinction to establish right out of the gate.

- Next, make certain to secure commitments from each team member up front. Ideally these commitments are secured in a group setting. The public commitment enables the rest of the team to hold the individual accountable. This means defining everyone's objective for the project, their responsibilities, how to best communicate with each other, key milestones, and hard dates to complete tasks. Make sure to restate upcoming goal deadlines as you wrap up your meeting with each team member. For example: "To ensure we are on the same page, here are the steps and due dates for our next meeting . . . " This is important. To avoid cognitive dissonance, the mind will do its best to honor the commitments we have made. Use this to your advantage in helping others meet their commitments for the project.

- Successful project management comes from building a system that helps drive completion and holds everyone accountable. In other words, you need an organized way to ensure follow-through. One of those organizational pieces is a regular update meeting for the project team. This could be as easy as a weekly status report where each team member shares what was completed for the week, whether they are on track relative to the planned completion date, upcoming tasks to complete, and obstacles they need assistance with. This kind of meeting and update helps everyone to share where they stand, encourages progress (by not wanting to admit to the team that they are behind schedule), and identifies obstacles the team can assist others with to complete the project (reinforcing a shared sense of ownership). This creates transparency and provides extra motivation to complete the task on time. People don't want to be viewed as the slacker in the eyes of their team or as the one holding the team back. The thought of having to provide a status update in a meeting where they say they have not completed their tasks will motivate or scare most people into pushing ahead and avoiding procrastination. This is a very powerful means of letting the system and team drive accountability versus you having to constantly crack the proverbial whip to ensure everyone completes their tasks.

- Another tool for driving completion of tasks is to build a project tracking report with the status of all the deliverables (on track, ahead/behind schedule), the committed completion date, and notes from each team member. Model the consistency you are looking for from the team by sending the tracking report out on the same day and time each week. For additional accountability, include all team members and the managers who have a vested interest in the end deliverable on the distribution list for the tracking report.

When dealing with an individual who has fallen off track or is resisting the plan, think about how the result of the project will impact them for the better. Communicate to them how this new reality (the completed project) will make their work life better.

To encourage commitment, ask what you can do to help them get the deliverable completed by the deadline. If you demonstrate a willingness to help with the solution, that can often assist those who are resisting to get back on track. If the issues persist, address the individual directly before elevating the problem and engaging their direct manager.

These basics will help you manage the majority of projects you will face in your career. If you aspire to specialize in project management or take your project management skills to the next level, look into some of the training platforms or project management certifications in your field.

EVERYTHING YOU TOUCH LIKELY WILL HAVE ASPECTS OF PROJECT MANAGEMENT.

Project management skills are important for all professionals to develop and possess. Everything you touch likely will have aspects of project management. Spend the time to manage these correctly, and your internal brand will benefit greatly as you enhance your productivity and professionalism.

ATTITUDE

We covered a positive attitude of taking ownership, but it's important to remember that a negative attitude, or being labeled a complainer, is a career killer. Be aware of how you are viewed within your team and within the organization. Do you complain a lot or associate regularly with those who do (guilt by association)? If so, this is not good for your professional brand and could potentially stunt your progress. Regularly assess your attitude (and your perceived attitude) and make adjustments as necessary to ensure that you are positively portraying yourself to your customer base.

ACCEPTING FEEDBACK

Another element that will help your professional packaging is to take feedback and criticism like a pro. In many cases the receiving party gets defensive at the hint of constructive criticism. This lack of receptiveness hampers the individual on two fronts. First, it demonstrates closed-mindedness. Ultimately that closed-mindedness will prevent this individual from growing and improving. Feedback is an essential part of the growth process, and without it development is stunted. Second, it can also damage a person's brand. This behavior demonstrates a lack of respect for the individual delivering it and can create the perception of a know-it-all who lacks humility and is unwilling to improve.

The appropriate way to handle feedback is to accept it and thank the individual for providing it. It is OK to ask for clarification to better understand the feedback, but do not concentrate on disproving the person delivering the feedback. The feedback is their opinion. It is another piece of performance data for you to assess; sometimes it will be valuable, other times it will not. Regardless, you should take the feedback in stride.

There will be situations when you may need to share additional information (factors the outside observer may not be aware of) to provide the feedback-giver with a complete picture of all the factors at play. Accept and acknowledge appreciation for the feedback, but find a nonconfrontational way to explain some of the other complicating factors that they ought to know. This is a delicate balance—you don't want to come across as though you are making excuses. Accepting feedback, along with taking responsibility for miscues, is part of taking ownership for your role. Your brand will benefit.

ENGAGEMENT

Another important packaging element for your brand is engagement. Engagement is very straightforward. Put simply, give everyone your undivided attention and you will be in good shape. In meetings, remove distractions like your cell phone to avoid the temptation of drifting away from the conversation at hand. Many of us (myself included) are guilty of multitasking, and it can be damaging. It gives the impression of lack of interest to the other parties in the meeting, and it limits your ability to digest what is being covered in the meeting. When I find myself drifting back to bad habits like checking my phone too frequently, I implement a personal phone ban and do not bring it into meetings.

Additional ways to engage are to ask thoughtful questions to show that you are listening and taking a genuine interest in what is going on around you. Strive to pay attention to others and what they are saying. Create a good habit here, and you will be able to pick up and retain great amounts of knowledge just by being present.

It is helpful to send positive signals of your engagement to other attendees by exhibiting cues of active participation through nonverbal acknowledgment and note taking. In meetings and conversations, jot down reminders to yourself (if necessary) and to reiterate your committed engagement to the topic at hand. The busier you become at work, the more valuable your notes will become, because it gets challenging to juggle all the responsibilities and remember everything that was covered.

THE LITTLE THINGS LIKE LENDING A HAND GO A LONG WAY TOWARD BUILDING MORALE AND HELPING YOUR BRAND.

Another way to engage within your organization is to volunteer to jump in on projects or in areas in need of support when help is necessary. This doesn't have to be a major project. It can be a simple thing like volunteering to help set up chairs (when you see your coworkers struggling) for a town hall meeting.

The little things like lending a hand go a long way toward building morale and helping your brand.

Acting like a professional is straightforward. The keys are to be disciplined and show up on time, be humble and accepting of feedback, and consistently engage others and the organization. If you regularly practice these basics, you will be poised to deliver positive brand impressions.

INCREASING YOUR LIKABILITY FACTOR

Most of our time at the office is spent with our customers (coworkers in this case). Given the proximity and the sheer amount of time we spend with them, the likelihood increases that we'll get too comfortable and violate an office norm or two. This creates unnecessary ill will toward you and your brand. As silly as it sounds, being liked plays a role in your career prospects. People are more likely to work, provide opportunities, and communicate more effectively with those they like. All things being equal, the likable person is going to get the benefit of the doubt over the unlikable person. We are unable to control whether someone likes us. However, we have ways to influence that, and the easiest way is to adhere to the basics of office etiquette.

Be accessible

Almost everyone in the office is busy. Many lesser employees will use this as an excuse to be difficult to pin down for meetings or engage with others in the office. Do not be one of them. This lack of accessibility is frustrating and makes it more strenuous for others to get their job done because of the interconnected nature of business. Business is still concentrated around people and relationships. Limiting your accessibility gives others a reason to get frustrated with you. You do not want the label of "not a team player" attached to your brand.

Make a conscious effort to have your office door open (literally and figuratively), and be flexible enough to attend meetings and respond to other requests as much as reasonably possible. It is polite and a sound practice. Think about what kind of impression you would have of a coworker if every time you stopped by their desk they seemed annoyed about engaging in conversation or answering a simple question. Likely, you will quickly establish a negative perception of this individual and take steps to avoid engaging them. Be accessible and open to others when they stop by your desk. Doing this is an easy way to avoid a reputation as a challenging person to work with.

Of course, there will be times when you do need to have a private conversation or quiet time to get work done. In those situations, it is completely appropriate to close your door or find a private conference room for working.

Respect others' space

When entering someone's office or cubicle, make sure to knock and get permission to "come in." You are entering someone else's personal space. Show that space and the other person the respect they deserve.

If someone has their door closed or is meeting with someone else, come back at another time. Interrupting comes across as selfish and disrespectful to others and their time. Obviously, if there is a time-sensitive emergency, ask permission to interrupt and explain the emergency.

Keep your own workspace neat and organized. The office is a shared space, and you don't want your part of it to be the eyesore. Additionally, it will give off a positive signal to others that you have your act together.

CUBICLE MANNERS

Be aware that other people are very close to you.

- It is easy for coworkers to get overly comfortable with this proximity and let their guard down. Once that happens, people start to have personal phone calls or openly discuss topics that are not appropriate in this public forum. These are annoying behaviors that paint your brand in a negative light.

Be respectful of your neighbors.

- Manage the volume of your voice when on the phone.
- Don't take calls on speakerphone.
- Use headphones if you are allowed to play music while you are working.
- Don't eat food at your desk. Just because you like the taste of what you are eating, it does not mean that your neighbors will enjoy the smell of your food.
- If you going to have a personal conversation, take that away from the cube "colony."

Greet others

When meeting people, practice good form with your greetings. A firm (not overbearing) handshake and eye contact give off a positive impression. Smiling also goes a long way in being well received. Use the other person's name when greeting them; people like to hear it. Our own name is generally our favorite word.

Be a team player

Working in a business means spending lots of time with other people, so it pays to be a team player. Be gracious and easy to work with. This means being generous with showing your gratitude for others when someone else does something for you. Don't be stingy with sharing praise. Compliment people when something has been done well. Share the credit willingly.

Participate in team and company activities. This means going out with the team for lunch or similar get-togethers. You want to be a reliable fixture in your organization. Showing up is a big part of it.

Use common courtesy

The basic common courtesies are even more important in the office. You will spend more time with your coworkers than with anyone else, and usually you are confined to close quarters. Remember things like using good manners, looking others in the eyes, cleaning up after yourself, and treating everyone with respect, regardless of title and role. The golden rule still has valuable applications today. Treat everyone the way you would like to be treated.

To avoid earning the reputation of having a bad attitude, do not be petty or speak ill of others. The office gossip and vent sessions are a trap. Being involved in that will only drag you down and prevent you from being successful. It will give you a pessimistic outlook and reflect poorly in management's view of you. If you have a criticism of someone else, address it directly to the person in a private and respectful manner. We will go deeper into conflict later in the book, but always strive to take the high road. Generally, a strong way to defuse the conflict is to admit the role you played in it as an issue and let go of grudges.

It might not hurt to take a manners course to improve your office etiquette. It is a great way to polish your people skills and create awareness of behaviors or tendencies you can improve upon.

PERSONAL AND SITUATIONAL AWARENESS

These etiquette basics will serve you well as a guide on what is appropriate and what is not. However, there are factors to consider that will alter the rules at play and force you to make adjustments and act accordingly. These two complicating factors are (1) you and your views, and (2) the situational elements at play.

Knowing yourself

After you have mastered the basics of office etiquette, you can graduate to more advanced personal marketing activities like looking inward to gain a better understanding of yourself, your tendencies, and the prism through which you view the world. We all have different styles and preferred methods for engaging others and engaging with our environment. Having a strong grasp on your personal tendencies will help you manage your effectiveness and your attitude in the office.

- **Communication.** Start by evaluating your preferred method of interacting for everyday activities. Do you prefer face-to-face interaction or written? What is the reason behind this preference? How does it make you feel when someone uses a platform that you don't like?

- **Issue Resolution.** Do you attack situations head-on or prefer to sit back and let the dust settle before addressing them?

- **Work Environment.** Are you someone who likes to come to conclusions on your own or do you prefer talking through complex situations with others?

- **Social Interactions.** Do big groups make you uncomfortable or do you crave the energy derived from a big group?

- **Learning and Obtaining Information.** Are you an auditory or a visual learner?

Understanding your preferences can help you manage your personal situational awareness. You will be able to quickly isolate reasons why you may be a little upset or frustrated when things deviate from your preferences. This kind of knowledge allows you to understand the sources of your feelings. Thus equipped, you can make more informed and measured responses to the daily stimuli. This in turn will help you to avoid potentially negative branding responses. Because inevitably we all will be agitated in the workplace. Solid performers find ways to get back on track faster and remain productive.

Also, use your self-awareness to alter your environment if it is less than optimal, or even potentially harmful. What are the preferences of your supervisor (aka your customer)? Are there any small adjustments/considerations that you can make to have a profound impact on how you engage with your customers? For example, if your supervisor prefers face-to-face communication while you prefer email, making the adjustment to correspond with your supervisor's preference will help you connect more efficiently and enhance your prospects for a more favorable relationship.

Your preferences can be quite telling as to the type of person you are, and how you like to engage with others and with your environment in the workplace. An awareness of your own preferences is powerful. It can help you more effectively navigate the daily rigors of your job, because once you have been in the workplace for a while, you realize how often soft skills come into play every day in the office. Each of these interactions, if managed correctly, can contribute immense amounts of social goodwill, improve your personal brand, and drive your career's well-being.

To augment your "self-discovery," it can be beneficial to take a personality test or two like those mentioned in chapter 1. Examine your results and what that says about you. These tests can help explain what motivates you and how you like to shape your environment. After reviewing, you'll likely discover the reasons why a lot of things upset you in the past.

On the DiSC profile, for instance, I am a "high D" personality and like to cut to the chase. That can be a strength, because I am driven to get things done; however, it can also be a weakness when dealing with others who do not share my preference for getting directly to the point. This drive characteristic pushes me to get to the result as quickly as possible. Others without a high D personality may need more time to warm up before considering conclusions. In my career, I have had to work to understand that sometimes you need to do the touchy-feely things before jumping right into the "business." It is important that I force myself to exchange some pleasantries and have a little bit of small talk before jumping into "the work." Then I can start to explain the context around the situation and the rationale behind a decision or recommendation.

Early in my career, because of this tendency, I received feedback that I was somewhat robotic and disconnected to others I worked with. In my case, I didn't have to become the most touchy-feely person on the planet to succeed. I just had to make strides to be more engaging on an interpersonal level to be effective. Having this awareness has allowed me to work better with others, thereby increasing my overall productivity.

A productive method to help diffuse your stylistic and preference differences is to explain your style to people as you work with them. This will benefit you in multiple ways. First, it is something personal to talk about (for those who don't like that kind of stuff, like me) to help connect with others, and it helps others to understand how you are hardwired. This type of declaration provides them with context and puts your style at the top of their mind. Likely, this will give you a little wider berth if you have a quirky approach, such as possessing a get-to-the-point style. But remember, just because you declare to others that you have a different personal approach, that is not a license to make zero accommodations to others. You still have to make progress on operating closer to the accepted social norms to put yourself in the best position to thrive.

Know your environment

As you move through the day, your environment is ever-changing. You need to account for those changes as you engage in the social situations you are presented with inside and outside the workplace. It is important to become hyperaware of the setting you are in and understand how that changes the dynamics of a situation.

By understanding the environment, it is much easier to navigate what the social norms are and how you should be behaving. Many times I have seen people make mistakes because they did not understand the environmental situation (myself included). Something that may be completely appropriate in one setting can be offensive in another. A perfect example of this is the work holiday party. Many people end up doing things that jeopardize their careers at these events because they only read a few of the social cues (party atmosphere and alcohol present) and neglect some other important factors (your boss and coworkers are in attendance).

To avoid misreading the situation, take time to mentally process where you are and what the expectations are. Verbally acknowledge these factors ahead of time to help ingrain them into your mind.

- Where am I? Work, school, bar, performance review meeting, social committee meeting?
- Who is attending? What kind of influence do they have on my career ambitions?
- Are there people in attendance who need to have a positive, professional impression of me because they can influence my career?
- What is the appropriate attire? The level of attire is a good barometer of the formality of the event. The more formal the dress code, the more formal the behavior. Expect higher levels of formality and decorum as the level of dress goes up.
- Do you understand your audience and their objectives, biases, and experiences? It is important to know your audience inside and out. Understanding what they bring to the meeting or social setting allows you to tailor elements of your response and message to connect with them more effectively.
- What is the objective of the event? The expectations of your behavior will be dramatically different at an off-site planning meeting versus an off-site team-building exercise. Know the objective and use that to guide your actions.

By taking a beat and understanding the situation, you can then think through what etiquette is expected of you socially and in general. If work or work people are involved, it is important to put your best professional foot forward.

Know your coworkers

Take the time to get to know your coworkers personally, whether they are direct reports, peers, or superiors. By knowing them and their tendencies you'll be much better prepared to work effectively with them, in both smooth and rough times. As you are getting to know your coworkers, take notes in private and have a profile on everyone you work with to accelerate your familiarity with them. This list should include personal facts about them (to help with future discussion topics) and work tendencies.

Keep this in a secure location and not on a work computer. The intent of this profile is very positive, but, unfortunately, it could be hurtful to others who don't know your intent if they see it, and it could even come across as a little creepy. When used the right way, however, these profiles will help you get to know your coworkers better and remember important facts (like names of family members). This information is powerful. If you can recall personal facts and truly know the other person, you will have an enhanced ability to connect with them.

Every day at work you will have opportunities to connect and reinforce your brand to your customers. Make the most of all work-related situations. Be mindful of acting the part of a polished professional, engage with your coworkers and environment, and pay attention to the quality of your work. If you manage this correctly, you will elicit positive emotional responses to the professional brand you are cultivating.

IDEAS IN ACTION

▶ Attributes highly valued in team members are: reliability, trustworthiness, competence, ownership, being a team player, and resourcefulness.

▶ The cornerstone to career advancement and professional success is projecting a professional presence consistently.

▶ Take note of what your manager wears to work as a guide to what is appropriate.

▶ Your tone, pace, word selection, and fluidity when verbalizing your thoughts will cause those around you to make judgments about your intelligence, your technical aptitude, who you are as a person, and your ethics. Choose wisely how you communicate.

▶ If you are the lead on a project, remind yourself that you are completely responsible for every aspect of the product delivered.

▶ Leverage credibility badges to enhance your personal brand.

▶ It is important to follow proper social and professional etiquette to help shape how you are perceived by your coworkers.

▶ Understanding your personal tendencies will help you manage your effectiveness and your attitude in the office.

10

Communicating in the Workplace: Marketing Your Brand

You've just started in your new position, and your company sends you to your first trade show to study the competition. As you approach a competitor's booth, the first thing you notice is that the business development manager manning the booth hasn't put much concern into arranging the marketing collateral and giveaways. They are sloppily laid out on the table, the company banners are crooked, and it only gets worse when potential customers stop to grab a giveaway and find out about the company. Instead of standing outside of the booth greeting potential customers with a warm smile and inviting body language, the manager is sitting behind his table with his feet kicked up and his head buried in his cell phone.

You've just learned a valuable lesson about what *not* to do. This company could have a stellar reputation and great marketing, but one misstep has negatively impacted the brand. You don't want to make the same mistake with the Business of You.

Marketing communication is a vast network of coordinated messaging aimed at building brand awareness that shapes customers' perceptions about products or services in the marketplace. Strong marketing organizations will use a host of platforms, such as broadcast advertising, direct marketing, branding, packaging, online presence, sales presentations, public relations, trade show appearances, and more. These communication vehicles are aimed at reinforcing positive feelings about brands and influencing customers' buying decisions. Simply put: If customers like what they see, they are more likely to buy it.

> *Broadcast advertising includes commercials or mentions delivered over TV or radio.*
>
> *Direct marketing is the use of mail, web, or telephone to drive sales without the use of a physical retail space.*
>
> *Brand packaging refers to the materials that wrap and protect goods and serve as a marketing vehicle to communicate with current and potential customers.*

The same applies to your career. Avoiding a simple misstep or a negative brand impression is why it is important to pay careful attention to all the elements of your personal marketing.

When you are in the office, you have a wide range of marketing communication tools you can use to promote and shape your brand's impression. Your interpersonal exchanges, email, phone conversations, meeting etiquette, reports, and casual downtime play a major role in how you are viewed by decision makers in the organization.

CUSTOMERS EVALUATE HOW PRODUCTS RELATE TO OTHER COMPARABLE PRODUCTS ACCORDING TO THEIR OWN MENTAL MAP OF HOW THE PRODUCTS FIT INTO THE MARKET.

Take a moment to think about the brand characteristics you are trying to convey on a regular basis, which you defined earlier. These are the brand-positioning elements you are looking to ingrain in your customers. In marketing, positioning is one of the greatest influencers on a customer's buying decisions.

> *Brand positioning is how a product, company, or service is positioned relative to its competitors in the mind of the customer.*

Customers evaluate how products relate to other comparable products according to their own mental map of how the products fit into the market. This means that if you can market your brand to convey your targeted characteristics (ambitious, self-starter, skilled at interpersonal communication, high potential, etc.), you are able to position yourself ideally in the eyes of the decision makers who have influence over your future opportunities.

The purpose of communicating is first to convey your ideas and information to others, and you must do this effectively if you want to rise in your chosen field. The secondary objective should be for all your communications to demonstrate a level of competence and professionalism that enhances your personal brand in the audience's eyes.

Your ability to convey information clearly and effectively will be tested numerous times each day in the workplace. Communicating well will pay some of the greatest returns of any investment you will make in your career. The pillars of effective communication are simplicity, timeliness, proper tone, and listening.

KEEP IT SIMPLE

The end goal of communication is to transfer information from one person to another. When communicating with others, your focus should be to clearly convey your message so that the recipient understands you. Remember this every time you are speaking or writing.

The foundational element of communication is simplicity. Clear, simple, and succinct communication allows the merit of your ideas to be displayed. When we attempt to look smart or use big words, we often lose the audience and fail in our intended purpose.

One way to keep it simple is to pretend you are communicating your message to a sixth-grader. Speak plainly, use common words, assume that the audience knows very little about the topic, and avoid jargon. Aim to transfer the necessary information from your mind to the other person's in the most direct manner possible. This applies to email and other written correspondence. Avoid long narratives and make bullet points your best friend. When used correctly, bullets can convey large amounts of information efficiently.

REPLY PROMPTLY: PEOPLE WILL NOTICE

In today's work environment, shorter attention spans and the need for instant gratification make it imperative that you are timely with your responses to correspondence and requests. When managers and coworkers send you a request and you can turn it around right away on a consistent basis, you will build a positive reputation. This is especially important early in your career. It doesn't take long for people to take note of how quickly you complete tasks and respond to requests. A reputation of being responsive carries some additional positive attributes (like possessing a high level of competence and strong organizational skills). Being responsive is an easy way to stick out in a positive manner, because many people in the workplace are not quick to complete other people's requests.

Strike a balance so that you don't get caught in the trap of back-and-forth communication rather than getting your work done. You still need to balance your priorities to ensure the highest-value activities are getting done first.

A solid rule of thumb is to not leave your office for the day without responding to every email and voice message you received during traditional business hours. If you stay true to this rule, you'll be able stay on top of your inbound communication and you won't have to constantly play catch-up because you are 100-plus emails behind.

DON'T WAIT TO COMPLETE THE REQUEST
BEFORE RESPONDING: RESPOND RIGHT AWAY.

Sometimes there will be requests or emails that will require you to do some research or that are waiting on a response from someone else before you can respond. Don't wait to complete the request before responding: Respond right away. Let the other person know that you will need to do some research or that you are waiting on a response from someone else, and provide an estimated timeline when you expect to complete the request. Be realistic on the estimated timeline and don't overcommit yourself. Build in a little buffer in your estimate to give you some margin for error.

Once you have responded, it's important to create a task or appointment in your calendar to remind you of the commitment you just made. That way you don't forget to follow up. This minor detail is a simple way to differentiate your brand in the workplace.

Also, make sure that you communicate intermittently between the initial communication and the completion of the project. If a response is going to take some time, provide periodic status updates if something changes or if you see progress. If you are still within the committed timeline, don't go overboard on the updates; just highlight significant changes or milestones. If the project or request has extended beyond the planned deadline, increase the frequency of the updates (potentially up to daily). This helps to reinforce the fact that you view this as an important matter and sends signals that you are working diligently behind the scenes. These quick status updates are important for a multitude of reasons: They demonstrate that you are on top of the request, they establish that you are a strong communicator and care about the request, and they kill speculation that you are sitting on the request.

ONCE YOU RECEIVE BAD NEWS, YOU SHOULD SHIFT INTO PROBLEM-SOLVING MODE RATHER THAN WASTE YOUR TIME WORRYING.

Timeliness of response is even more important when it comes to delivering bad news. Most people tend to avoid conflict and will naturally delay or avoid delivering it. This strategy only makes the situation worse. In addition, you have more time to build it up in your mind, which can compromise your ability to deliver the news in a measured manner.

Once you receive bad news, you should shift into problem-solving mode rather than waste your time worrying. That means you will need to take a moment to collect the facts, review your potential options or alternative solutions, and prepare a game plan for delivering the news. Then, connect with the parties involved who need to hear the news as soon as reasonably possible. Be empathetic but matter-of-fact with your delivery. A common mistake in the workplace is delivering bad news with an overly apologetic tone. Playing off that kind of delivery, the receiving party often makes a bigger deal of the situation or even sees that tone as guilt, meaning that you are the cause of the disruption or issue (which may or may not be the case).

Often when bad news is delivered in a timely fashion and with the correct tone, you will be surprised at the response. Most people will be reasonable, understand the facts, and shift their focus to where to go from here. Occasionally, you may receive an angry or unreasonable reaction (sometimes warranted), and that will make you think twice about delivering bad news in the future. You cannot control how others respond to bad news. All you can do is respond swiftly and thoughtfully, and by doing so, put yourself in the best position to succeed.

TACTICS FOR TIMELINESS

You're trying to establish a reputation within your organization as someone who is diligent about responding to requests. This means quick turnaround times to emails and voicemails. Doing this will also help to create a positive halo effect around your work because you will be perceived as diligent. Next are a few basic guidelines on how to enhance your responsiveness.

- To establish your personal standard for responding to calls and emails, review your company's policy on responding to correspondence. If you want to be a high achiever, make sure to be more effective than the company standard. That standard is the minimum expectation for all employees. The minimum just doesn't cut it if you want to accelerate your climb.

- A good rule of thumb is to have zero messages waiting in your inbox and voicemail box before your leave work for the day. You don't have to be perfect with this, but if you strive to accomplish this every day (and achieve it most days), you will be viewed favorably.

- Make sure you are responsive to everyone. A common mistake is to respond only to "important people." This harms you on two fronts. You will not garner universal support and praise (managers often ask all types of coworkers their opinions when considering internal candidates for promotions), and you are missing an opportunity to develop a strong habit of responding quickly to all requests.

- Create folders to file emails that you may need to reference later but have limited use for right now. Many times, individuals are well intentioned and keep those emails in their inbox, which only clutters things up and makes it more difficult to get to a zero inbox.

- Implement a system to ensure you complete your follow-ups. Note if additional work or communication is required after your email response. Outlook is a great tool for flagging emails or setting tasks and appointments. There are also hundreds of applications that can help you stay organized on your follow-up. Find your own method. The most important thing is that you have a system that puts you in a position to not miss a follow-up.

- All of us can be guilty of avoiding an email—because of who it's from or what's being requested. Fight off the urge to procrastinate, and attack your email head-on.

- Remove clutter from your email. Proactively mark junk emails that come in as spam. These fill up your inbox and cost you precious moments. Additionally, take yourself off distribution lists for reports and other communication that you do not receive any value from.

- Don't rush your responses. Many employees who grasp the importance of responding quickly make the common mistake of responding in haste and producing a poor product. Move quickly and with a purpose, but do not rush and make sloppy mistakes like misspellings or incoherent thoughts.

WATCH YOUR TONE

Like it or not, our minds will try to subconsciously find ways for our feelings to manifest, and often that will come out in the tone we use. You can manage your tone by being aware of situations where you are likely to slip up, and by proofing your correspondence from a tone perspective.

Tone is the attitude, spirit, or feeling that is derived from a piece of writing or speech.

Tone is a powerful tool that often gets overlooked during communications. This is surprising, due to the level of influence it can have, both positive and negative. Tone, when harnessed correctly, can amplify your impact. However, even the best choice of words, written or spoken, can be misconstrued if your tone is incongruent with your intended message.

Often tone betrays us when we are rushing—perhaps producing a tone that's too direct; other times underlying emotions bubble up to the surface in our correspondence—when our tone might convey unhappiness or disdain about our role in a project.

Remember: Emails live forever

Be on alert for the signals of a situation when your tone is more likely to get compromised. The times when you are upset are the highest risk. Think about situations and triggers that put you in a negative state of mind. Do you have major pet peeves that could set off negative feelings? Are there certain people that get to you, for whatever reason? When this happens, step back and process what is going on. Make yourself assume positive intent, and focus on what you are trying to convey in your correspondence. Yes, that can be difficult. But when you make a quick negative association with a situation or person, that is the lens you view through: negative and distorted. Negativity then becomes associated with everything about that situation or person, and in a lot of cases that is not fair. Then your correspondence is corrupted and you communicate with an underlying negative tone that ends up being counterproductive.

There are different elements to pay attention to when assessing tone, depending on whether the communication is written or face-to-face. The overwhelming majority of written communication today is through email. When assessing an email response, you will be evaluating the words and some of the addressing elements: Did the writer take the time to formally address the receiver of the email and sign off? Are others CC'd on the email, and if so, who and why? Does the last sentence lead toward finding a resolution or opening an argument?

When talking to someone in person, your tone through nonverbals is being evaluated as much as your words. Pay attention to your voice, posture, and the environment of the conversation, as they play a big role in the evaluation of the message. The advantage of in-person communication is that you will be collecting real-time feedback. If you see body language change dramatically into an angered or protective stance, then you have struck a nerve or your tone is amiss.

When evaluating your words, try not to use absolutes unless they are 100 percent reflective of the situation. What I mean by absolutes are words like *always*, or phrases such as *every single time*. Typically an absolute is an exaggeration, and it raises the stakes of the conversation unnecessarily.

Along the same lines, including definitive demands, such as *you must*, or *required*, creates the wrong tone. Alternatively, frame the request in a more positive light:

> "You need to play nice with the sales team" versus "Engaging the sales team in a more collaborative approach will yield far greater results and foster a healthier environment. This can be accomplished by . . . "

When commenting, focus on the action, activity, behavior, or feeling instead of the person. You are trying to correct something specific, and when you make it about the person, it turns up the stakes unnecessarily. A sign of focusing too much on the person is the overuse of the word *you*. If you see a lot of *you*s in your correspondence, that is likely a sign that you are focusing too much on the person and not the action, activity, behavior, or feeling.

EMAIL AND PHONE BEST PRACTICES

Most of you will say that you already know etiquette for the phone and email, which is likely true to a certain extent. But in most cases, that etiquette is based on norms for personal use, which is more relaxed. Little things like using a professional greeting when answering the phone or removing distractions while engaged in a phone conversation can have a big impact on how you are perceived.

Email considerations

There are special considerations that come with the use of email in the work environment. Email is a great tool, but it often is misused and tone is easily misinterpreted. A common mistake is to jump right into requests or news too quickly. Take the time to provide the necessary context. When making a request of someone, take a sentence or two to lay out the background and purpose behind the request. It helps the other person to understand the bigger picture; this allows them to naturally transition and process the request.

When communicating complex requests or confrontational content, add a sentence or two at the end to bring the tone of the email back up to a more collaborative place. A positive upswing that encourages collaboration can help to steer the potential response into a more positive direction. For example, a concluding line like "Do not hesitate to reach out if you have any questions or if we need to talk through this further" sends a positive message. The reader will feel that you are reasonable and supportive in helping them through this request or conflict in need of resolution.

Email best practices

Most communication in the business place now occurs through email. These days, the majority of people in the workforce are tech natives. However, that comfort with the commonplace leads to misuse of this tool. Being overly casual and relaxed in your correspondence will ultimately paint you in a less-than-professional light. Respect email as a medium that will project the professional reputation you want associated with your brand.

SNAP JUDGMENTS ARE BEING MADE ABOUT
YOU EVERY TIME YOU SEND AN EMAIL.

When you send an email to a coworker and customer, it is a formal communication in a professional environment. Treat it as such. Delivering the content like you would a text message to a friend shows very little respect for the audience (and looks unprofessional). Proofread your emails and be grammatically accurate. Like most things in the workplace, snap judgments are being made about you every time you send an email. What kind of impression would you like to leave with the other person? Think about that every time you are preparing an email.

ASSUME THAT ALL YOUR EMAIL TRAFFIC IS
BEING MONITORED, BECAUSE IT IS.

Do not send anything inappropriate at work. I shouldn't have to say it, but it is worth mentioning because of the potential downside. It does not matter if it is a friendly joke to a trusted friend. Assume that all your email traffic is being monitored, because it is. A joke is not worth losing your job over. To put it simply, when it comes to emails, do not send anything you would not want published.

STRUCTURAL BASICS TO FOLLOW WHEN CRAFTING EMAILS

- When addressing an email, use a professional greeting and closing. This helps to give a more formal structure to your email correspondence by conveying a level of respect and organization. Starting your email off with the recipient's name personalizes it and elevates the perception of your request when compared to the rushed blank-heading version of the email that lacks the person's name.

Signing off with "Regards" (or a comparable equivalent) before your name reinforces the same positive elements.

Pat, Thank you for all your efforts organizing the breakout sessions for the annual conference. The extra practice sessions with the facilitators really paid off. You were an instrumental part of making this a big success. Regards, Lukas

- Use your signature block in every email. It makes it easier for people to track down your contact information, and it presents a professional appearance.

- Subject headings should be informative and let the receiver know exactly what the message is about. Be thoughtful with your subject heading—it is like the title of a book. Accurately sum up the purpose of the email. If you are changing topics on an email thread, change the subject heading to match the new subject.

- DO NOT USE ALL CAPITALS. See? It feels like someone is yelling at you.

- Use simple formatting and professional fonts. Similar to building your resume, don't get overly creative with your backgrounds and font colors. The default settings work just fine. You may think it is a creative expression of you; you are wrong. It is a distraction and looks hokey.

- When using email, do everything possible to avoid long narratives. Take the time to prepare a concise, careful, and accurate message. Being quick and to the point will give your content the best chance of being read and remembered. With the ever-shrinking attention spans out there, your long email is less likely to be read completely.

- Bullets are effective for conveying large amounts of information in a concise manner. This breaks the information into a much easier form to digest.

- Don't overuse the high importance designation. If every single email is important, how does someone determine which ones are most important? Over the last decade of my career, I have sent no more than ten high-importance emails. My mantra is that if it wasn't important, I would not be sending it. Those who always send these emails look foolish and a lot like the boy who cried wolf.

- Clearly communicate what the expectations and next steps are. If you need a response in a certain time frame, spell out those expectations. Be crystal clear on what you need from the other person. The same goes for informational or low-importance emails. If you don't need a reply, start the email off with: *FYI – No action required.*

- Be mindful of whom you include on emails. You don't have to CC the world. Before adding someone to an email chain, ask yourself if it would add value for the individual and the organization.

- Be very aware of your tone when using email. In email, tone is often misinterpreted, because reading tone in an email is a tough exercise and open to interpretation. That is why it is important to be gracious in your email correspondence. Consistently use please and thank-you. Ask more often than you tell. Take the time to walk in and out of a point. This way the reader gets context and does not feel like you are being curt.

Here are a few additional tips to manage your tone in emails:

- Before you send an email, make sure that you are showing the appropriate level of respect to the receiver of the email.

- Tone is arguably the most common pitfall in email correspondence.

Reread your email, focusing solely on your tone. Is there anything there that could be misconstrued or viewed as demanding?

- Many people don't realize they are giving off the wrong tone in emails. If the topic is an emotional one, try your best to conduct this conversation in person or over the phone.
- Avoid humor. The degree of difficulty for executing humor over email is very high. Humor and sarcasm do not translate well in an email.

If you treat email with a level of respect and as a professional platform, you will be in great shape. Follow these guidelines religiously early on, and writing emails like a pro will become a habit.

TELEPHONE

Over the phone, the nonverbal cues such as facial expressions and body language are not available for the other party to assess. This places a greater importance on the use of tone and pace, and on being thorough and specific in your explanations.

Avoid telephone land mines

Like email, the telephone is a place where we can get a little too comfortable. When we're comfortable, we let our professional guard down and act in a more informal way that may not be constructive to the development of our professional brand. Before we jump into the best practices, let's review a few common pitfalls.

HUMOR

As with email, be cautious with the use of humor. It is much more difficult to be in on the joke without the nonverbal indicators. If you have a strong relationship already in place and know the other person's baseline and vice versa, it becomes easier to inject humor into the conversation.

SPEAKERPHONE

Avoid using speakerphone at all costs. There will be times in a group setting in someone's office or conference room where it is appropriate. The use of speakerphone comes across as being disengaged to the other party. It is a complete no-no if you are in a cube colony or an open area.

BE MINDFUL OF YOUR NEIGHBORS

Do not be the loud person in the open area or the cube colony. Be aware of the volume of your voice and what you are saying. If it is a privileged conversation, find a private place to take the call. Remember, everything you say in the public setting will be used against you. Make certain you are portraying yourself in a positive manner. This means always use a professional tone and avoid profanity and personal calls.

DISTRACTIONS

Be 100 percent committed to the conversation at hand. Do not attempt to multitask. Things like answering emails or fiddling with online searches impair your ability to fully engage in the conversation. You may think you are being stealthy and the other person will not notice, but you are not, and your lack of engagement will show. The other person on the phone will feel like you do not value their time and attention.

The same goes for eating or chewing gum during the conversation. Do not do it. The sound of chewing or swallowing is annoying to hear on the other end of the line, and it sends the wrong signals.

Phone best practices

Our world is shrinking, and business is being conducted on a global level. Transactions happen now without either party meeting face-to-face, often making the phone the most intimate form of communication the parties will engage in. Given this extra importance placed on the phone's role in establishing relationships, it is critical to put yourself in a position to best cultivate strong relationships. Here are some tips for successful phone correspondence.

- Take a few breaths before answering the phone and prepare yourself for the transition into a new conversation. A common mistake is bringing a frustration from a different situation into another conversation. All you are doing is digging yourself a bigger hole to get out of and being unfair to the other person on the line.

- With caller ID, you most likely already know who it is before answering. A common mistake is assuming the call is coming in for a negative reason because of who is calling and your impression of them. It may very well be a negative call, but give the conversation and the relationship a chance. If you go in expecting the negative, it will be a negative discussion no matter what. Do not underestimate how your attitude can shape the direction of a conversation.

- Your company will likely have guidelines on how they would like the phone answered, so make sure to fit your greeting within these guidelines.

- Good posture will make a difference in the sound of your voice and your energy level. An ancillary benefit is it reinforces your good posture so that it becomes more of a habit and second nature to you.

- Smile. This is an old sales-professional trick. This helps your body emit a more positive-sounding tone. In addition, smiling will help trick the rest of you into believing you are happy.

- Confirm understanding. For particularly difficult content or a deviation from the norm, take the time to confirm that the other party fully understands the information you are trying to convey. You will need to secure a verbal confirmation, since you will not be able to read their nonverbals.

HAVE A SYSTEM

Make sure to manage expectations and have a plan for managing your incoming calls. If you are in a role that does not require you to be immediately responsive to customer or coworker calls, develop a system where you are only returning voice messages at certain times. For instance, in the role that I hold today, I only return calls at 9:00 a.m., 1:00 p.m., and 4:00 p.m. Adjust the times and frequency accordingly for your role and the demands on your availability. The only way this will be successful is if you state that policy on your outgoing message and notify your team of your approach. This will make you more effective in your day. The distraction of having to respond immediately breaks up the flow of your workday and monopolizes valuable time that could be spent doing something else. This same practice should be used for email correspondence.

The phone is a regular part of most people's jobs. Master the basics described here to make sure that your professional brand is maintained and strengthened in your organization.

MANAGE YOUR TONE

When communicating directly with your voice (by phone or in person), the same principles apply as in written correspondence.

Your voice is an instrument that will play a role in both phone and in-person conversations. The volume of your voice and the pace at which you speak can be played up or down for effect.

For example, as the stakes of a conversation are raised, many of us will tend to speed up the pace of our speaking or increase our volume. This creates a feeling of amplification of feelings and emotions, because often the other person feels this and starts mirroring the same changes in volume and pace. This amplification can be an effective tool when used at the right times. However, in this hypothetical situation your objective is to secure alignment with a coworker in a different department that has not worked well with your department in the past, so a calm, slower pace of communication is going to be more effective in conveying your message. If you feel your tone getting away from you and deviating from the "script," take a moment, acknowledge your change in tone, and correct course by softening your voice and pace, deescalating the situation.

Take note of other tendencies you have verbally when you get agitated. Sometimes your pitch will get higher. Be aware of these "agitators" so in the moment you can manage them and correct course if you are unnecessarily raising the stakes of the conversation.

WHEN YOU'RE FACE-TO-FACE

For face-to-face communication, all of the same principles apply as in written and voice communication; but when face-to-face with someone else, the nonverbal layer gets added into the mix. Your posture, facial expressions, overall body language, and how you are positioned in the room carry significant weight with how your tone is received by the other people involved in the conversation. To avoid escalating the stakes with your body language and nonverbals and to open the lines of communication, pay close attention to the following details.

Environment

The environment can have a subtle but impactful influence on a conversation. Barriers like tables and desks create a physical and emotional boundary between people communicating. Try to manage the communication environment by removing barriers (like a desk) so that you have an unobstructed view of each other. In a conference room, where you cannot move the table, most people will sit on opposite sides, which creates a feeling of competition. Instead, try to sit next to each other at a corner of the table. It provides a small barrier, but also offers a greater opportunity for you to connect. Removing barriers can make people feel slightly vulnerable at first (with nowhere to hide), but helps to create an atmosphere of honesty and trust that will help the dialogue.

Posture

Put thought into your posture. In a conversation, it helps to have a welcoming pose. This means open arms (not crossed), making yourself appear vulnerable and encouraging of discussion. The same goes for crossing your legs. Crossing your arms and legs are protective stances that can have a similar impact as having a large conference table between you and your audience. Use friendly hand gestures when engaging in conversation, and don't point at others when referring to them. Instead, aim your hand at them with your palm up toward the sky—a much more inviting gesture. Also, be aware of how you use your confidence poses and territory-claiming body language during conversations. If the other person is showing a position of vulnerability, you may need to turn these confidence body-language elements down a couple of notches to make the other person feel comfortable.

Situation

Be aware of how your tone and body language fit with the message you are delivering and within the environment. Throughout every day you will be confronted with a multitude of situations. These situations can range from extremely sensitive and challenging to trivial. Depending on the variables at play, the significance of the message, timing, the other person involved, and the setting of the conversation, you will need to vary your approach accordingly.

Make sure your choice of words, tone, and body language are assets in these situations. In some cases, it pays to be bigger and bolder with your body language and more forceful with your tone. Other circumstances will require you to turn those aspects down and create more of an engaging disposition. Unfortunately, there is no set standard for the best approach. This is a skill that you will need to develop a stronger feel for and be able to adjust through trial and error.

WHAT IS YOUR OBJECTIVE?

A consistent theme throughout this book has been to suggest starting your interactions by establishing your objective(s). Once that is clear, consider the subject matter that will be covered and how the other person may feel during this dialogue. Is this a discussion that will generate a significant level of emotion (positive or negative)? Or is this a small matter that will not register?

Also, consider the other person involved when assessing the potential response. Is this an individual that has a difficult time accepting feedback, or is this a sensitive topic for the individual? If the answer to either of these questions is yes, you should lean toward a gentler approach than usual when it comes to your tone and body language.

GIVING FEEDBACK TO A DIRECT REPORT

In a potentially emotionally charged environment like providing constructive feedback to a direct report, certain considerations will need to be taken in order to make the session a productive one. Given the nature of the content, you need to provide this feedback in a private and safe space. Your tone should model the environment you are trying to build. A calm, lower-pitched tone in your voice and welcoming gestures will accomplish this. Imagine the damage that would be created with a loud, aggressive tone. Even with a nonconfrontational approach at the outset, the other person may get defensive and take a more combative stance during the conversation. If you feel the tone going that way, pump the brakes and bring the tone back, for the benefit of both parties.

A common mistake in situations like providing constructive feedback is to dance around the feedback and "soften the blow." When you do not clearly address the issue, you are cheating yourself and the other person. You are not providing the person with the necessary feedback to improve. And without that, you may ultimately need to terminate their employment—making you culpable in their failures because you did not give them the full opportunity to improve. To be successful in this difficult conversation, let your body language and tone be the calming factors as you matter-of-factly address the issues head-on.

Timing

There is never perfect timing, but try your best to take timing into consideration when communicating with others. Be aware of when and where you are delivering a message. The perfectly planned and executed conversation can be undermined if it is happening at the wrong time. For this, you need to be sensitive to others and what they are going through. For example: Your coworker has just wrapped up a long and daunting presentation for a project she has been working on for a couple of months. Right after that presentation is not the best time to have a one-on-one sit-down to discuss how her phone etiquette is impacting her neighboring coworkers. The individual is apt to be emotionally depleted and will likely generate a negative emotional response and resistance to your feedback. Give that person a day or two to decompress to avoid immediate resistance, and to help minimize her potential resentment by viewing you as insensitive.

It does not happen often, but there will be a time and place for you to show your passion or motivate others through raising your voice and being extremely direct with your words and tone. If you are traditionally very measured and balanced with your voice and tone, using a contrasting style becomes a powerful tool that you can use sparingly. It will catch people by surprise and carry more weight because it is out of character and demonstrates the gravity of your words.

Communicating and managing tone is an art form. You will gain a better feel of what works well with practice. Create a feedback loop by recording yourself when possible. When appropriate, ask for feedback. As you get better at using tone and understanding your style, you will be able to summon and apply the appropriate variables when necessary.

LISTEN

Listening is by far the most important part of communication. Effectively obtaining information and letting others express themselves is the bedrock of communication and establishing fruitful relationships. Listening takes work. It requires you to take the time to hear others out completely and pay close attention, so that you fully understand what the other person is communicating verbally and nonverbally. Strong listeners are better positioned to establish trust with others and strengthen their personal and professional relationships. Throughout this section we will outline the foundational elements to enhance your listening skills.

Create a safe environment

If the other person in your conversation feels they are in an unsafe environment (meaning a place where they will be mocked, have their words used against them, or shared with others), they will not be open and candid. Your actions will set the stage for this environment. If you have put in the time to build a relationship and established trust by treating sensitive conversations with confidence, you will have solid footing in creating a safe environment and having a reputation as trustworthy. If this is a relatively new relationship or you are attempting to restore trust, this will be an uphill battle.

To cultivate a safe environment for communicating:

- Acknowledge the objective of the discussion so there is no confusion or suspicion of an ulterior motive. Example: "My objective for our conversation is simple. I want us to get to a positive place and repair the damage done from the dispute last Thursday. For us to heal from this dispute, I believe we need to have an open and honest discussion of what transpired and how it impacted us."

- Make sure the other person knows this is a discussion between you two only and nothing will be shared with others (and mean it!).

- Start out by making yourself vulnerable. This means being honest and sharing your feelings. This helps to give the other participant permission to do the same.

This prep work is an important piece of the listening process. Only in a safe environment will people feel comfortable enough to fully express their thoughts and feelings. That allows you to get deeper into topics and make true progress.

Time

Provide ample time for the other person to share their thoughts. If you do not lay out enough time for the conversation, the other person may feel rushed or shortchanged. If you have a hard stop schedule-wise, make sure to note it in advance so all parties can manage the conversation accordingly.

Avoid interruptions

Avoid the temptation to interrupt. For us talkers, it can be hard to sit back, because we want to engage in the conversation. As the other person is sharing their thoughts, participate in active listening. Acknowledge with nonverbals and by restating your understanding of what was just said during natural breaks. In an ideal scenario, you should let the other person share their thoughts first. This is done for several reasons. It gets the dialogue rolling and lets your conversation partner feel active right out of the gate. Also, it helps to calibrate where the discussion needs to go and items that need to be addressed.

In addition, find a venue for the conversation that limits the number of outside potential interruptions.

Lock in

Remove all distractions and look squarely at the speaker. This means putting away your phone and turning off your monitor if you are at your desk. Shut the door of the office or conference room. Your objective in the conversation is to gather as much information as possible when the other person is talking to you. As you are listening, make assessments:

- What, exactly, is being said? How is it being delivered? How are these words different from what you expected to be said, and why?
- What is the other person's body language telling you? Pay attention to facial expressions and posture. Are the nonverbal cues congruent with the words being stated? If something is amiss, share your observation with the other person to get a deeper understanding of what is going on.
- What is not being said? Was something important omitted? Why would that be omitted?

Actively listen

Active listening requires you to engage with the other person. When they are speaking, demonstrate that you are listening with your body language (leaning forward, nodding along at points) and with verbal cues (yes, uh-huh). To confirm that you fully grasp their message, restate in your own words your understanding of the other person's thoughts. Take time to digest the message and reserve judgment. Once you have done that, you will be able to respond appropriately.

Many people struggle at this foundational element of the communication process. That is why developing the reputation as a strong listener is a great asset for your professional brand. People will trust you and engage with you more often. This enhances your relationships, making you more effective in the workplace. And as others come to you, you will access more information, keeping you dialed into the organizational happenings.

FINALLY: TOOT YOUR OWN HORN

In today's hypercompetitive job market, you must promote your brand to help yourself stand out relative to the competition. Internal promotion of your skills and accomplishments requires a delicate balance. Too much self-promotion is off-putting and can alienate your customers. However, if you strike the right balance and tone, you are creating positive brand impressions by controlling the message.

A GOOD PERCENTAGE OF US DO NOT FEEL COMFORTABLE WITH INTENTIONALLY POINTING THE SPOTLIGHT AT OURSELVES.

Strike a balance

This is a skill I struggled with mightily early in my career (and honestly, I am still not overly great at it today). A good percentage of us do not feel comfortable with intentionally pointing the spotlight at ourselves. The key to striking that right balance is to be subtle and to present the facts in the normal course of business updates and reports. It must feel organic and relevant to the topic at hand.

Track your results

Early in my career I had a manager who advised me to track what I was doing and the results of those efforts. At first, I did not fully grasp the point of the exercise. I was very busy at the time, and I thought my manager was asking me to do unnecessary work. From my perspective, I already had a ton on my plate and did not have time to document and track progress. In addition, I was uncomfortable with the thought of "self-promotion." My manager had worked in several other large companies, however, and explained the importance of tracking your personal progress, tracking results, and highlighting your accomplishments. Because when all is said and done, no one else will document your accomplishments for you. To take that a step further, outside of your close work circle, most people will have no clue what you do on a daily basis. Given those facts, you can see why it is important to take a proactive approach to creating brand awareness in your organization.

My former manager could not have been more correct on the importance of tracking your efforts and results. Set a regular schedule (weekly) to jot down your accomplishments for the week. Block off time on your calendar to make sure you do this task. This list should consist of wins, disasters adverted, and positive contributions that helped the overall good of the organization. Additionally, you should track key measurements that are the direct result or are influenced by your efforts. Analyze these regularly, looking for both positive and negative trends that you can focus in on to address and correct quickly. This exercise of documenting activity and results helps you in several ways.

- You'll be exponentially more effective in preparing for your end-of-year performance reviews. You will be able to prepare quickly and not forget about accomplishments that were done in the first quarter and would otherwise be a distant memory.
- You'll be locked and loaded for presenting your case for a promotion or raise to your boss.
- You'll be prepared for your job search if you elect to pursue other

opportunities. Having a library of your greatest hits available makes the usually painful task of building a resume much less painful.

- You can respond quickly to correct unfavorable trends, improving your performance and contribution to the organization.

Highlight your wins

Now that you have a regular practice of tracking and documenting results, the hard part starts—using that information in a productive manner. The use of your information should be an organic part of your regular meetings with your supervisor. For your weekly (or regularly scheduled) meeting you should have agenda topics for updates. During that time, you should highlight the wins for the week, missteps, concerns, and items you need assistance with. By tracking your good news, you will have a lot of content to highlight. However, it is not beneficial to present a false sense of success. That is why you must be balanced and share the negative elements also. This is beneficial for several reasons. You demonstrate your grasp of the business, you show confidence, and you address issues head-on to avoid them getting worse over time.

By sharing these trends and feedback, your manager can see the progress of your activities. I'm not talking about shameless self-promotion here. I have worked with plenty of people who focus on explaining how good they are instead of working. This method can be damaging to one's career prospects. Often those employees get marginalized. Their onslaught of self-promotion works against them because most people tire of hearing about all of the great things they are doing, or begin to discount the accomplishments out of fatigue.

If you present your information correctly, your manager will appreciate the updates and progress reports because it keeps him or her in the loop. Also, it doesn't hurt to serve as a friendly reminder of all the hard work and contributions you are making to the organization.

Make it public

Another way to organically demonstrate your impact is to share the trend reports that you are tracking, not only with your manager but also with involved team members, when relevant, on a regular basis. This helps to reinforce your value and, if presented regularly (with good or bad results), you will not come across as a glory hog. An ancillary benefit of making these results public is that they will provide additional motivation for you to perform well, because the last thing you want out there is a report with negative results.

Just as TV and print advertising are the platforms for companies to shape how their customers view their product and organization, the way you communicate serves the same purpose for you and your brand. With every interaction, email, and phone call you are shaping coworkers' and managers' views of you. Considering that those impressions will impact a large part of how your skills and competence will be evaluated, shouldn't you be thoughtful about how you present yourself?

IDEAS IN ACTION

- ▶ The pillars of effective communication are simplicity, timeliness, proper tone, and listening.

- ▶ The foundational element of communication is simplicity. Clear, simple, and succinct communication allows you to showcase the merit of your ideas.

- ▶ A consistently quick and effective response to emails and other requests will help to firmly place your brand in good standing with your customers.

- ▶ Be on alert for the signals of a situation when your tone is apt to become compromised.

- ▶ Being overly casual and relaxed in your correspondence will ultimately paint you in a less-than-professional light. Treat email as a formality, and respect the medium so that you project the professional reputation you want associated with your brand.

- ▶ Effectively obtaining information and letting others express themselves is the bedrock of communication and establishing fruitful relationships.

- ▶ Internal promotion of your skills and accomplishments requires a delicate balance.

11

Operational Marketing: Preparing for Success in Your Day-to-Day Responsibilities

When you see a well-produced television commercial, it is easy to discount the work behind the scenes. To produce that slick-looking advertisement, there was extensive customer research conducted (competitive landscape, demographics, spending habits, hot buttons, market-positioning analysis, etc.). Multiple script revisions were made to dial-in words, visuals, and sound effects. And that is not a comprehensive list of the prep work that happens before the actual filming and editing of the advertisement. A well-produced commercial is a powerful tool for companies. It shapes the consumer's opinion of the company and its product. When executed correctly, it drives the purchasing decision and helps the company grow.

You can harness the same influential power to elevate your career prospects in the workplace. The difference is instead of a tightly produced commercial, you are packaging your performance in the platforms of meetings, presentations, and the way you lead projects. Every day, decision makers watch how you perform, and they are evaluating your competence and future potential.

A professional who excels at meetings, presentations, or leading a project is held in high esteem; those skill sets engender a positive association with the person's internal brand. This positive association leads to more opportunities and being positioned to rise through the ranks quicker. These individuals have mastered operational marketing.

Operational marketing is based on delivering service that exceeds customer expectations. Think about a restaurant that you return to regularly. In many cases, your decision to return is not made solely on the quality of the food. One of the main reasons people become "regulars" is because the service experience is phenomenal. What creates that kind of experience is making you feel at home and loved. That means the staff knows your name, gets your order right, and does everything in their power to make sure you are enjoying yourself.

WHEN A PROFESSIONAL IN THE WORKPLACE EXCELS AT MEETINGS, PRESENTATIONS, OR LEADING A PROJECT, THEY ARE HELD IN HIGH ESTEEM, AND POSITIVE ASSOCIATION IS ESTABLISHED WITH THEIR SKILL SETS AND INTERNAL BRAND.

You need to be doing the same with your career. When you are in meetings or presenting, managers and coworkers should feel that positive association with you and your skill set. When you see someone excel, it appears to be second nature to the individual, which, looking from the outside in, can be intimidating. In most cases, it is not. That smooth delivery is the product of significant preparations behind the scenes. These are skills that can be developed. And they are important ones, because like the slick TV advertisement influencing a purchase decision, you can influence decision makers into giving you the opportunity to advance in your career.

PRACTICE, PRACTICE, PRACTICE

If you are looking to consistently produce at a high level in the workplace, look no further than the sports world, where the hours of preparation outnumber game-time hours significantly.

It takes a fair amount of natural talent to get to the highest levels of sports. That doesn't mean, however, that those born with talent always make it to the top. Instead, the individuals who typically "make it" are the ones who fully subscribe to concentrated practice and complete preparation. The reason is because an actual game makes up such a minuscule amount of time when compared to the work leading up to it. Those who thrive in the preparations are most likely the ones to succeed.

Corporate America is no different—the vast majority of our leaders aren't the ones with the most natural intelligence or talent. Instead, they're the ones who put in the time on the "practice field."

Every meeting, presentation, and interaction, after all, is a chance to improve and shape how you are perceived in the organization. Wouldn't you practice if you had a big game coming up? Work should not be any different.

> **THE VAST MAJORITY OF OUR LEADERS AREN'T THE ONES WITH THE MOST NATURAL INTELLIGENCE OR TALENT. INSTEAD, THEY'RE THE ONES WHO PUT IN THE TIME ON THE "PRACTICE FIELD."**

After my brief professional baseball career, I adopted the following mantra for my business career, and it has been a game changer: You do not have to be the smartest person in the room; however, it pays to be the most prepared.

This focus on preparation stems from a sports background of practicing and preparing for the games. Everyone loves the games. It is fun and exciting to show up and play in front of big crowds. The individuals who ultimately thrive in games are the ones who, beforehand, are doing everything physically and mentally to succeed. Especially the non-glamorous things, like working hard when nobody else is watching. Think back to a time when you didn't prepare for a sporting event, recital, performance, or presentation. How did that turn out? Poorly, I imagine.

The same thing happens when you don't prepare for the simple things at work, like a meeting with your boss. Most people will show up to a meeting with their boss and wing it. The unprepared person will hit some of the most important problems and topics; however, they will likely forget a couple of questions they should have asked. The discussion will bounce around and have no logical flow. If the manager asks a probing question, this person will likely stammer through an answer, without having conducted any research or put in much thought on the topic. What does the manager see when someone shows up for a meeting and just wings it? An unorganized, unprepared employee who doesn't respect the manager's time. The employee might come across as a shallow thinker, because the employee was not able to string together a cohesive response to simple questions.

This is a basic interaction that is often taken for granted. It can be very damaging to your career prospects if not managed correctly. By not preparing, you are establishing a poor reputation with your manager. Remember, this is the person who likely has the greatest impact on your chances to advance in this company. How many other opportunities to shine are you not taking advantage of?

Imagine how different the meeting could have gone if you had spent just a few minutes to prepare. You could have:

- Written out a basic agenda

   This would have kept you organized, provided a logical flow for the meeting, ensured that you covered every topic, and showed that you are respectful of the manager's time.

- Taken a moment to research and think about each topic around your agenda

   This would have helped you develop fully formed thoughts on these topics. You could have tried to find answers to the questions your manager would likely ask. What are the challenges surrounding these topics? What might the manager want to know about it (price, progress, etc.)?

Even a brief few minutes spent on preparation can have a long and lasting impact on your performance, how you are perceived, and your career. Now think about how many other opportunities you have daily to better prepare to display your talents and shine like a polished professional more consistently— thus sending your career on a different trajectory.

Throughout the remainder of this section we will outline a framework for how to prepare in the workplace, and we'll demonstrate the framework in action in some everyday work situations.

THE KEY ELEMENTS OF STRONG PREPARATION

Define the objective; scout and research; develop a game plan; practice reps; mentally prepare; game time; and leverage feedback loops.

Define the objective

As Stephen Covey covered in his great book *The 7 Habits of Highly Effective People*, begin with the end in mind. In sports and in business the objective is the same—to win. In business, winning is not as easily measured as in sports with a scoreboard. Winning can come in many different forms. That is why it is valuable to define the winning objectives up front so you can focus your efforts on the correct ones.

Start by defining the broad, overarching end goal of the event, meeting, presentation, or project. This is your primary objective, and the majority of your preparation efforts should be aimed at accomplishing this objective.

Then drill down into your ancillary objectives. These are typically smaller, like changing a perception or demonstrating organizational skills. Chart these objectives, as you will try your best to accomplish as many of them as reasonably possible during your planning stages.

For improved alignment with your objectives, try to get into the mind of the customer or audience for your work product. Think in terms of what the end users are looking for from your output. What makes them tick? What are their end goals? Are there things that you would like to accomplish with this group to add to your list of objectives?

Once you have the objectives pulled together, use others to help dial in and test them. Get a couple of opinions from trusted sources (coworkers, end users, mentors, etc.) on your objectives.

As with defining your personal mission statement for projects, meetings, events, or presentations, it is important to have a clearly defined picture of what you are striving to accomplish. This target, or targets, will serve as a guiding force for your efforts. Refer often to your objectives list to stay on track with your preparations. An organic way to weave this in is to review the objectives after returning from a break. This can be a good transitional warm-up for the activities and reset your focus and efforts.

Another way to stay close to your objectives throughout the preparation process is to be able to see them. Writing your objectives on a whiteboard or somewhere prominent will help serve as a continual reminder of what you are determined to accomplish. Small guideposts like this are key in preventing you from deviating too far from your mission.

A clear set of objectives is the foundation of your preparations. As you go further into your preparations, you will often refer to this groundwork that you've laid down.

Scout and research

In the business world, one of the most commonly underestimated elements of the preparation process is the gathering of information about your audience or the customer for your work product. In sports, teams will fly evaluators to competitive teams' games and watch film to scout their competitors' strengths, weaknesses, and tendencies, in order to gain any slight edge over the competition.

Think about the leg up you can have if you just take a few moments to consider who will be attending your presentation or receiving your work product. If your manager has a preferred style or hot button about certain things, wouldn't it make sense to tailor your presentation or product accordingly? For example, what if your manager hates PowerPoint presentations? How do you think your pitch would be received if you presented it in PowerPoint? Your manager would likely be put in an unfortunate frame of mind, and that would spill over and could negatively impact his or her thoughts on your pitch.

Do some investigating to establish facts, objectives, and potential impediments, so you can develop a tailored presentation that will give you the edge you need. Scouting reports to assess the involved attendees, team members, customers, and the tools at your disposal will reinforce a strong foundation for your project.

SCOUTING REPORTS

To help you better understand those who play a big role in your future (managers, influential coworkers, customers), a wise investment of time is to build a scouting report of things they like and dislike. Pay attention when these individuals provide feedback or comment at meetings or after events. Themes and preferences will start to develop. Over time you will collect enough information to help you optimize your presentations and tailor pitches toward those influential individuals' preferences.

Just remember to be discreet with your personal files. Your "scouting report" is an innocent and well-intended research product; keep it confidential.

ASSESS THE PLAYERS

Before every meeting or presentation, take a moment to evaluate the attendees and figure out their perspectives. What are their roles in the organization, and what are their objectives? Consider how your message or potential comments will change or impact them. Are there topics the attendees are sensitive to? In most cases, the last thing you want is to provide opportunities for the discussion to dwell too long on one of those sensitive areas and completely derail the mission of the meeting or presentation (unless the objective is to tackle this sensitive topic). Ultimately, the key is to be mindful and tailor your message to the audience to put yourself in the best position to succeed.

IDENTIFYING YOUR INTERNAL ASSETS

In your network or in the office there are likely many resources at your disposal to improve the quality of your work product. Leverage these tools as much as possible. They will help you to produce a higher-quality product in a shorter time frame. Within your company there are likely a lot of intelligent people who have produced significant pieces of work, so be efficient by avoiding having to learn from scratch or re-create something that has already been developed.

Awareness plays a big role in your ability to identify needs and resources to utilize. It is important to uncover what assets you have at your disposal, but it's also important to have self-awareness of your areas of expertise and limitations. Then find areas to round out your strengths and weaknesses when you are working on a project.

Consider the subject matter. Are there experts on that subject within your company and network? How could they play a role as you prepare for your project or presentation? When you engage others for assistance, show the appropriate level of humility and appreciation. You are asking for help, and they can make your life, as it relates to this project, exponentially easier. Their expertise will accelerate your progress and elevate your work product. Before you start a project, assess what resources you can access that could assist you with this specific task:

- **Tools.** Tools can come in many different forms. A tool could be as simple as a corporate template for presentations, or as comprehensive as a resource library on customer research.

- **Team Members.** Is there a team member who possesses experiences or talents that could assist with this project? Don't limit yourself to only those who succeeded. Team members who failed at a similar project can also be a valuable resource. In many cases they can provide insights on why something went wrong and major pitfalls to avoid.

- **Friends and Former Colleagues.** Assess your network outside the business in the same way you'd assess the one inside the business. In my case, design and layouts are one of my weaknesses. One of my best friends is a graphic designer and has helped me many times. In exchange, I have helped him with advice for managing and leading challenging personalities on his team. This informal bartering system of skills has benefited both of us and enhanced our careers.

- **Mentors/Personal Board of Directors.** Obviously, your personal advisors will have great experience for you to pull from. The other benefit is to use this group as thought partners to bounce ideas off. Their seasoned perspective is an invaluable asset.

You can now see how a strong network can be a powerful tool for you and your career. Your relationship-building efforts from chapter 8 will pay great dividends. Just remember that if you utilize the talents of others, be prepared and willing to do the same for those who help you. It is a two-way street, and most productive professional relationships are those that give freely back and forth.

Develop a game plan

With your objectives defined and research conducted, you are ready to develop your game plan. Your game plan should consist of the tactical elements you are going to use to accomplish your objectives. For a meeting your game plan will consist of several elements. Your agenda is the backbone of your plan. It outlines the topics and the sequencing of the topics you want to discuss. Put careful consideration into what is covered, when it is covered, and why it is in your agenda.

An agenda is a powerful tool that should be used for every work activity and meeting. That means preparing an informal agenda when you are having a simple one-on-one meeting with your boss, subordinates, or a coworker. This simple task will aid you in accomplishing your objectives and ensure that you cover the topics you need to cover in the meeting. It will also demonstrate your organizational skills to your colleagues.

Part of your game plan is to prepare for the unexpected, and it should include a plan for contingencies if something goes awry. Say, in a meeting, the discussion veers off track to a topic you would like to avoid. For instance, are you prepared if "Bob" vents about his department's lack of visibility in the roll-out process? Or if you are giving a presentation and the AV goes down? These types of things happen more often than we might expect. How would you respond? If the AV goes down, be prepared with paper copies of the presentation, or know your presentation so well that you can deliver it without the AV.

It is impossible to prepare for every potential imperfect situation. However, if you have a plan and have prepared for the major potential negative scenarios, you will be able to respond like a pro and put yourself in the best position to succeed and limit the disruptive impact of whatever went wrong. Ever notice that when one of these "bad" things happens to a top performer, they seem unrattled and plow ahead? Often it is because they have already prepared for this kind of "disaster" scenario.

Practice reps

Regardless of the task, what are the chances of you executing a given task perfectly on your first attempt? Extremely low. That is why people practice everything ranging from fire drills to walking through a big presentation. Take the time to work out the kinks before getting in front of an audience. This shouldn't be limited to just presentations, either. Practice what you are going to say before you attend meetings. Even one simple practice run-through will help you to have a smoother delivery and more confidence, resulting in an enhanced profile in those meetings.

One of the most common mistakes here is practicing the wrong way. Many people will read over what they are going to say, without attempting to re-create the environment for the "performance." For a more impactful practice, do what you can to re-create the live situation. Use the tone and energy that you would in the "real" situation. When practicing, mimic the little details. Will you be standing or sitting? Visualize the people who will be in the room. Who will you be looking at when you are speaking? These types of considerations can go a long way toward making you feel more confident in the real-life situation.

Practice enough times to become comfortable. Embrace the concept of diminishing returns when it comes to practice. There is a point you cross when you have gone too far with practicing, where your performance can come across as overly rehearsed and lacking energy.

The same goes for memorizing your statements. Memorize your general thoughts and the messages you are looking to deliver. If you attempt to memorize every word, it is easy to get tripped up when you slip up on a single word.

Mentally prepare

One of the easiest tricks to performing at a higher level is to mentally prepare before going into a meeting or presentation. Block off three to five minutes beforehand to get your mind right. Take a few breaths and review your game plan for the meeting. Remind yourself of your overarching goal for the next meeting or event on your calendar. This will get you focused on what you need to accomplish instead of bringing your other meetings or responsibilities to the task at hand. All too often we jump from meeting to meeting and don't make the mental transition, ultimately undermining the quality of our attitude and performance in each situation.

For peak performance, consider when you operate at your best. What time of day are you at your best? This is the time you should use for production or scheduling important presentations or meetings. Put yourself in a position to shine. Additionally, think about what helps to relax you and put you in the right mind-set. Does a quick walk outside help settle you? Have you ever noticed that a basketball player does the same exact thing before every free throw? Routines and patterns help put a player in the right frame of mind to replicate a successful performance.

Game time

The performance should be the fun part. You have put in the work; now it is time to trust your preparations and shine. Be present and focus on the moment. Don't get ahead of yourself. For example, when you are presenting, zero in on the current slide and give it everything you have. Staying in the moment will allow you to provide your best effort, rather than being distracted and focusing on future content or areas that you are not yet able to influence.

Leverage feedback loops

Soon after you have completed your presentation, meeting, or sales call, it is important to take a moment to review your performance. Whenever possible, record them (using video or audio). It can be a bit awkward to watch or listen to yourself on tape, but the perspective it provides is invaluable.

Earlier in my career I had a sales position—which is not my forte—and I struggled at first. I decided to record myself and dissect the calls to find where I had opportunities to improve my delivery and process. This process was eye-opening and humbling. After only a couple of weeks of reviewing my performance and applying the necessary modifications to my calls, my results improved dramatically. It was no coincidence. Those successes built upon themselves to help create some positive momentum for me in that role.

One of the most important factors in a personal and professional execution is a feedback loop. Your feedback loop should cast a wide net. This means going beyond recordings to peers, managers, direct reports, skills assessments, and performance measurables. A well-rounded feedback loop will provide you with the information necessary to assess performance and gauge your progress. To create your own personal platform to collect feedback, structure it to collect input from multiple areas and various levels of your professional network.

- Clearly lay out your goals for the feedback (to get better). Give the provider of feedback permission to be candid. Most people will say you did great. If they do that, ask for one thing you could have done better or differently.

- Create a formal structure to collect feedback regularly (quarterly meetings, mentoring, etc.).

- Find times to randomly check in between formal sessions to gauge your progress.

- Take the time to evaluate your own performance (see below).

- Record yourself making presentations or phone calls.
  - Pay attention to how you deliver information.
  - Do you use common verbal pauses?
  - How is your tone?

- Review old project materials.
  - Why was this project a success?
  - Knowing what you know now, what changes could have made this project more successful or impactful?

- Difficult situations or conversations are typically fertile opportunities for learning experiences. After a difficult situation or conversation, collect the facts and dissect what created the tension.
  - How did you handle the conversation?
  - What is your role in contributing to the issue?
  - What is the other party's role in this issue?
  - Where were the communication breakdowns?

The first step in the feedback loop is to collect the information and identify opportunities for enhanced performance. Then the important work starts. This means distilling the feedback and identifying a couple of key areas to focus on to improve your performance. Do not attempt to take on too many improvements at once; your attention will be spread thin and you won't be nearly as effective.

Also, the enhancement opportunities should be prioritized by the potential impact they can have. The higher the potential impact of the opportunity, the higher the priority of that opportunity. From there, develop an actionable game plan to work on improving in this given area. This follow-through is the most important part. You have laid down a significant chunk of work leading up to this point, and if you don't put a plan of action in place and act on it, this effort will be for naught.

Sports offer a great comparison. Think of how world-class athletes push themselves every day to get better, stronger, and faster. The same strategy applies to the business world. Ask yourself if you are making the effort to be smarter, more effective, and more well-rounded in the workplace.

We began this chapter by talking about professionals who execute their daily responsibilities and handle disruptions in stride, while making it look effortless. Their work product is excellent, and their personal brand is held in high esteem. These are the individuals who excel in the workplace and are given those opportunities to grow and advance. You can be one of these professionals if you consistently leverage the practices behind preparation. If you put in the work behind the scenes to put yourself in the best position to succeed, the sky is the limit. The secret is that you have to be willing to put in the work.

IDEAS IN ACTION

- You do not have to be the smartest person in the room; however, it pays to be the most prepared.

- The key elements of a strong preparation are: define the objective, scout and research, develop a game plan, practice reps, mentally prepare, game time, and leverage feedback loops.

- Prepare for the unexpected. Your plan should include contingencies in case something goes wrong.

- Practice reps are the secret to consistently performing at a high level. Take the time to work out the kinks before going in front of an audience.

- When it is time to perform, trust your preparations and shine. Be present and focus on the moment. Don't get ahead of yourself.

- Every client interaction, meeting, and presentation is a chance for you to demonstrate your skills. These are your "games" and will be the basis for how managers and coworkers evaluate you.

12

Strengthening Your Relationships

For the Business of You, it is important that your customers (managers and coworkers) are happy with the relationship, continue to buy your product (your gainful employment), and desire to purchase more (giving you promotions and additional compensations). And as you climb the ranks, your ability to work with people becomes even more important for getting things done. Leadership—formal or informal—is all about compelling groups to operate at a high level. That is why employees who flourish are typically the ones who excel in establishing deeper and more productive relationships with the people they work with, which allows their teams and project groups to produce at a high level.

To take your customer relationships to the next level at work, you will need to invest in those relationships to maintain and strengthen them. That investment is made through the skillful management of more advanced interpersonal skills. Those skills include: providing honest feedback to others without alienating them, resolving conflict, influencing others, and becoming fluent in the nonverbals going on around you.

In this chapter, we will show how to develop some of these more advanced and challenging strategies for relationship building and maintenance in the workplace.

Peter Drucker, who has been described as the founder of twenty-first-century management, said it best: "The purpose of business is to create and keep a customer." That is why in business, once a well-performing company gains a customer, they do everything in their power to retain that customer. Client acquisition is extremely expensive and time consuming.

Client acquisition is the process of persuading customers to purchase your product and/or services.

Strong organizations invest heavily in cultivating strong customer relationships, with the aim of retention. They invest in various resources:

- Account managers for questions and issue resolution
- Customer satisfaction surveys and other research
- Regular communications, such as newsletters
- Customer appreciation gifts
- Creating games or status based on usage

Similarly, in order for the Business of You to prosper, comparable investments need to be made to cultivate your customer relationships.

HONEST CONVERSATIONS

The foundation of deep and impactful relationships in the workplace and in your personal life is having open, honest channels of conversation. Unfortunately, we are all guilty of not confronting reality at times, because we naturally feel the urge to avoid tough conversations. Confronting reality can be challenging and makes most of us uncomfortable. There are a multitude of reasons for this feeling of unease: aversion to conflict, not wanting to hurt others' feelings, worry about hurting the relationship, and so on.

Starting at a young age, we are taught to not say anything if we do not have anything nice to say. This leads many of us to be hesitant to provide critical feedback, because we fear hurting someone else's feelings. Also, we are submitting to our natural setting of pain avoidance (the pain, here, is having to engage in a difficult conversation). It's natural to not want to hurt someone else's feelings, but it is the wrong response. By not providing the necessary feedback, we are doing the other person and the organization a disservice. The key is to provide feedback the proper way, so everyone benefits. That can be challenging. Providing feedback so that it is not received as an attack, but rather as a gift intended to help improve performance, can be accomplished through honest conversations.

Honest conversations occur when we come from a well-intended place and provide feedback and opportunities for improvement that will help another person. That intent is completely based on improvement and is not about knocking someone down a peg or two. The content of honest conversations is pragmatic, focusing on performance and behaviors, not on ego. When done correctly with positive intent and the right focus, the feedback helps the person receiving it to improve, and ultimately it deepens the relationship between the two parties involved. And when everyone involved becomes comfortable with having honest conversations, the ensuing trust will translate into more effective cooperation and collaboration between the parties.

Be honest

The first level of honest conversations is providing feedback actively in real time. Being critical or voicing a contradictory opinion requires a delicate balancing act of maintaining respect while providing insightful feedback from your vantage point, which helps all parties land on the best possible resolution. If you are going to be taken seriously in the organization and not viewed as part of the office décor, sitting in the room quietly watching, you will need to voice your opinion in active discussions with your superiors. Doing this correctly demonstrates confidence and respect. You do not want to be labeled as a "yes man" or "yes woman" who will follow the leader blindly off the cliff without saying a word. But if you raise objections too frequently, you will establish a negative reputation as a contrarian or naysayer. If you deliver a fact-based opinion respectfully, you will be in a good position to manage this delicate balancing act.

It is paramount that your intent is pure. It should not be about winning an argument or proving someone wrong. Your mind-set for engaging in the dialogue where you will provide feedback should come from a place of improving the discussion or resolution by providing the facts, insights, and opinions from your vantage point.

Equipped with a well-intended focus, you can then shift toward assessing the situation and the appropriate way to engage in the conversation. At first, take note of the venue of the discussion. Is this a formal presentation? If so, it is probably not appropriate to provide feedback on the spot. Take notes on the topic you want to discuss further and follow up with the individual one-on-one or during a planned question-and-answer session. Is it a public forum or a one-on-one meeting? In a public setting where there is an audience (especially if leadership or your supervisor is in attendance), ego is likely more at play. Use caution in this setting, because the person receiving the feedback is more likely to default to a defensive posture. This tendency to get defensive can be magnified by the level of ownership and pride the person presenting has with the project or thoughts. Take extra measures to demonstrate respect (compliment elements that you agree with and assume positive intent with your questions) when in a public venue and providing constructive feedback. That will elevate the tone from the outset if the discussion is delicate in nature.

Try your best to understand where the presenter is coming from. Is this an idea they just came up with, or is it a passion project they have spent large amounts of time on? If you know the presenter well, are there any personal biases that have shaped this person's stance or perspective? You should always tread lightly and respectfully in sensitive areas, but you can see how considering some of the factors previously mentioned will provide you with a solid gauge for determining whether to use additional caution to guard against an emotional response.

Once you have a strong grasp of the surrounding environment and factors at play, you can initiate the feedback process. Start by asking clarifying questions. Make sure to challenge your assumptions and clearly understand what is being presented. The worst thing you can do is to be critical of something that doesn't exist—because you jumped to conclusions. You can look foolish and damage your relationship, all at the same time.

Here is an example of how to provide feedback in a productive way by initiating a fact-based dialogue.

I was in a meeting with our marketing team and they presented their idea to introduce a low-cost product. Our brand is firmly positioned in the premium product category, so an obvious concern I have is that this low-cost product could potentially erode the brand equity we have established. Therefore, I asked the following question:

How has the potential impact to brand perception been evaluated?

This question is powerful because it safely starts the dialogue on the topic without being accusatory. Additionally, how the question is framed here assumes positive intent (that the impact has been considered). That is so much more productive than a negative approach. A common misstep here would be to ask a biting question that makes the questioner feel smart and makes the receiver of the question feel under attack. That is the quickest way to shut down a productive dialogue. I have witnessed leaders of organizations ask questions like this:

Did you even consider the damage this was going to cause to brand perception?

See the difference? You can easily see how being on the receiving end of this negatively framed question could quickly put a person on the defensive.

Once you have opened the discussion in a positive manner with your initial question, cite the facts as you view them (acknowledging this is your view) when raising objections. Don't simply say, "I don't like your stance." Your objections should be well-thought-out facts and insights from your experiences. Systematically lay out your thoughts on the matter. To avoid being viewed as completely undermining the individual, make sure to acknowledge the areas where you agree to help establish a commonality. Lay out the facts as an equation of positives and negatives that have shaped your stance. This shows that you put careful thought into your position and that you are evaluating the decision, not the person. That is an important distinction. At no time should the other person feel like this is a personal attack. Focus on the facts and the ultimate objective of the project or decision.

This dialogue should go both ways. After you present your thoughts in a concise and clear manner, make sure that the other person understands them. Then open yourself up for comments or criticism by the other person or the broader group. You could say something like . . . "That is how I see things from my vantage point. Does that make sense to you?" Or, "Are there any flaws in my logic, or any additional thoughts anyone has on this matter?"

This approach shows humility and demonstrates a willingness to get to the correct answer without worrying about authorship.

If the conversation starts to veer off track, topic- and productivity-wise (which can happen often when you have competing viewpoints), take a moment to reset the conversation by asking the other person(s) what they believe is the end objective, and share your view of the end objective. Anchoring back to the objective is a great way to avoid straying too far from the end goal. Additionally, this can reestablish a positive trajectory, as both parties should find some common ground on the end objective, and some of that goodwill should spill over into the rest of the conversation.

If you stay true to the intent of improving the end outcome, demonstrate humility, focus on the facts, and have a willingness to hear others out, you will be in the right place to have a constructive dialogue that will result in better outcomes and relationships.

Have courage

Throughout your career you will need to provide planned feedback to a coworker, manager, or subordinate. Planned feedback can range from conducting a performance review to addressing a team member who is not pulling their fair share of the load with a project. Delivering candid feedback is an important skill for a contributor at any level. It is how you get the most out of your coworkers and your relationships in the workplace. One of the reasons most don't excel in this area is because people often shy away and say that you are doing "great" instead of having an honest dialogue about performance. That approach lacks courage and helps no one. Let's look at some of the important preparation elements required to provide planned feedback effectively.

KNOW THE PERSON YOU ARE DELIVERING THE FEEDBACK TO

Is this a person who is open to feedback? Do they have certain sensitivities? Take these into consideration when planning what you say and how. These sensitivities do not mean that you change the topics you are covering. It means that you are mindful of these "emotional land mines" and will proceed with extra levels of respect in those areas.

RIGHT PLACE, RIGHT TIME

During this conversation, the other person may feel vulnerable. That is why it is important to start out by creating a safe environment for the other person to receive constructive feedback.

The right environment consists of two things—location and timing. Constructive feedback discussions should take place in private. If you are going to be treading on topics that are highly sensitive to the other person, think about having the discussion in a neutral location like a conference room instead of your office.

Try to avoid inopportune times to deliver this information. A less-than-ideal time could be right after some other bad news (which makes it feel like the sky is falling) or right after great news (bursting their bubble). Unfortunately, there is not always a perfect time to deliver constructive feedback. Sometimes you will just need to plow ahead, but try your best to avoid undesirable timing.

MEAN IT AND LIVE BY IT

Plan on some small talk to warm up the room and the discussion. Is there a shared interest or something that would help the other person feel comfortable? Use a topic like that to help them relax and to get the conversation off to a rolling start.

Once you transition into the actual purpose of the meeting, start by saying this is a safe place and everything that is said stays in this room. The most important part of this statement is to mean it and live by it. Verbalizing this helps to provide a sense of safety and helps to prepare the other person for the seriousness of the upcoming conversation.

Another way to show respect and create a feeling of safety is to ask permission to have an open discussion about the potentially uncomfortable topic that you are planning to cover. As you jump into the topic, it can be helpful to start out with an example to reframe the conversation. For example, "My objective today is to talk through a couple of elements that I believe are potentially limiting your effectiveness. My goal is to have an open and honest discussion on these elements to help set you up to be more successful in the future. Do I have your permission to talk about these opportunities to enhance your effectiveness?"

Be concrete, be balanced

When you are delivering the feedback, remember to focus on the behaviors and not the person. Do not generalize. Use concrete examples. Make sure you can provide multiple tangible examples of the behaviors you are discussing. Sometimes feedback is difficult to hear. That is why it is important to provide multiple examples so it cannot simply be dismissed as a freak thing or situational response. This will help the person receiving the feedback to digest and believe it. Be mindful not to go overboard and provide too many examples, because this can have the negative consequence of the person feeling like they can do no right.

Be direct, honest, and do not mince words. You should be businesslike with some empathy sprinkled in. A word of caution: A common mistake is to attempt to soften the blow by diminishing the core of your feedback. It is OK to be kind, but do not compromise the heart of the feedback that the other person needs to hear. You may think you are sparing this person's feelings, but you are compromising their ability to be successful in the future by not delivering the message to them straight.

THE SANDWICH METHOD

One of the old-school methods that still has some value, under the "delivering challenging content for beginners" heading, is the sandwich method. This methodology is where you share genuine appreciation for the individual, then cover a development opportunity, and close with what the future would look like if the development opportunity gets adopted. Just like a sandwich, the meat of the content is sandwiched in the middle. It is important that the sandwich is hearty and you don't skip out on the "meat" of that sandwich.

Let's see how the sandwich method works. Start out by communicating honest appreciation to the person receiving the feedback:

> *"Tim, we appreciate your great work ethic and everything you have contributed to building our new-hire training process. A perfect example of this is the late nights you put in last week to make sure we were prepared for the upcoming class."*

The important thing here, just like providing feedback, is to make sure to share a tangible example so the feedback lands and has meaning (instead of feeling hollow).

The next step in the sandwich method is to deliver the feedback focusing on the behavior.

> *"Your ability to connect interpersonally and persuade others on projects could be enhanced if, during interactions with others, additional time was spent to understand them, their vantage*

point, and their objectives. In multiple settings [share the actual situations witnessed], I have witnessed interactions where your drive to complete a task quickly and at your own pace leaves others feeling somewhat steamrolled and not invested in the end result. While this direct method can make you effective in the short run, it is a contributing factor for why you had less support from other team members and had to work those late nights last week."

The important thing to notice in this example is that we focused on behaviors and results, and not the person (*your ability* and not *you*).

Close with how the future could look better if the new and improved behavior is implemented.

"Tim, those relationships and your effectiveness will increase exponentially if the time is taken to ask questions to understand your colleagues' concerns and hesitations with change, before proposing the actionable next steps. Take the time to ask them questions like:

What are their objectives for this project?

What concerns do they have?

If they were managing the project, how would they proceed?

These types of questions will help you connect with others and help them feel connected with the project. If you can consistently implement this simple tweak to your approach, others will be more likely to embrace your ideas. And this will increase your ability to persuade and drive positive change within the organization."

The closing comment shows what the potential future looks like, as a way to encourage the individual to embrace the opportunity for improvement. The most important part of the close, however, is to clearly outline what steps need to be taken. To be effective with this closing, you need to provide a well-defined, actionable path to obtain that brighter future, so the other person is positioned to act on this feedback.

To reinforce the behavior and recognize respectable progress, make sure to catch the person doing things the right away. Thank them and tell them they are doing a great job improving. This will strengthen the relationship and set the stage for more productive feedback sessions in the future.

You will encounter numerous people in the workforce who will avoid providing feedback and having honest conversations, out of fear of harming relationships. The problem is, without these conversations you are hampering your ability to connect with your customers/coworkers on a deeper level. If managed correctly, honest conversations will help you to cultivate deeper and more productive relationships and enhance the desirability of your brand and career prospects.

CONFLICT RESOLUTION

A major part of business and your career success revolves around people and relationships. Just as in real life, the workplace is full of conflict. Conflict in the workplace comes in all shapes and sizes, ranging from the minor disputes stemming from someone speaking ill of someone else behind their back, to major issues arising between departments due to competing objectives. Large or small, these conflicts can fracture the bonds of relationships between you and your internal (coworkers and managers) and external (vendors and customers of the company) customers.

It is important as an aspiring leader to build your skills in managing through the conflict to repair cracks in relationships. Top performers and leaders strengthen their customer relationships in the midst of conflict by swiftly resolving issues to keep the work effort moving forward unimpeded by the collateral damage caused by the conflict. Individuals with this skill set continue to get things done despite tough situations, and they bring people together in the bumpiest of times. That is one of the main reasons they have advanced in their careers.

As you climb up in the ranks within your organization, you will be put in the position to resolve conflicts more frequently. Most people in the workplace fall into two camps: those who create the conflict, and those who make every attempt to steer clear of conflict. Conflict is a great place to flex your professional and interpersonal muscles. If you are going to have to get in the middle of a conflict regularly, you might as well become proficient at managing it so you are not bogged down and kept from conquering your other responsibilities and objectives. Here are some points for working through these types of situations.

Consider the good guy/good gal syndrome

When you jump into conflict resolution, remember that almost everyone sees themselves as the good guy/good gal in the conflict. Each party has collected the facts and data points that confirm their positive standing. When a situation requires elements of mediation, it helps to consider this, and to understand that you will need to help everyone (yourself included) view the situation from a different vantage point.

Remove emotion and be the bigger person

First and foremost, leave emotion at the door. It is easy to get wrapped up in the emotional components and go down a path of escalating the conflict instead of resolving the dispute. Strive to be the calming force in the situation. It will often require you to be the bigger person first. These situations tend to be emotional. Do everything you can to present a calm and even-keeled approach.

- Slow your rate of speech.
- Use a softer tone.
- Be aware of your feelings.
- Use inviting and open body language.

If you catch yourself getting wrapped up in your emotions and contributing to the conflict, stop, and remind yourself of why you are doing this: to get to a resolution. Competitive people (myself included) tend to see conflict as a competition. If you fall into that category, you will need to fight the urge to "win" the argument. It is very easy to fall into the trap of thinking winning is about being right. That is wrong. Winning is getting to a place where everyone feels comfortable moving forward, and not vanquishing your "opponent."

Be prepared—confer with yourself first

Before you engage in conflict resolution, have a conversation with yourself. Ask the following questions:

1. What is the end goal or mission here?
2. How will your conversation progress the cause and add value to the situation?
3. What results do you want from this difficult conversation or meeting?
4. What needs to be done from your side to end the conflict?
5. What needs to be done from their side to end the conflict?

Preparing and understanding the answers to these questions will help you focus on the situation from all perspectives and take a logical approach, instead of an emotional approach, to resolving the conflict.

Show respect

Typically, in conflict, as emotion creeps in, the involved parties are less than respectful of each other. Start things off on the right foot by reestablishing the courtesy and respect that all parties deserve. Thanking everyone for meeting with you and stating up front that you want to understand their perspective will go a long way in setting the correct tone.

Respect the involved parties' emotions by focusing your phrasing and discussion around behaviors, actions, or your feelings, and not the people involved. Remember, when it feels like a personal attack, it is easy for someone to get defensive and derail the progress toward resolution.

Put safety first

Set the stage by saying that the meeting is a safe place and the discussion will not go outside of the room. Honor that commitment, or trust will be completely broken. Make sure the venue is private, and that the room is set up to foster communication by limiting the number of structural barriers (like tables or chairs) between parties.

Let every involved party be heard. All participants need to feel like they can share their side and express their feelings. Having their say is an important part of the resolution process. This exercise is therapeutic and lets others digest issues from a different perspective, which helps everyone take ownership of their respective roles and contributions in this conflict.

Take your time and state the facts

Often it will take time to get the conversation rolling in a productive manner. Early in the dialogue, acknowledge what has been going on. For example: "Ever since our last project I have felt a tension between us that has hampered our ability to work together."

Get the problem out on the table so it can be addressed head-on. In that acknowledgment, avoid any assignment of blame.

As you continue with the conversation, state the facts as you know them. Do not express an opinion or make a conjecture about those facts. Encourage others involved in the conversation to share the facts as they know them. Talking through the facts helps to understand the variables and perspectives at play. In most cases, this helps each person better understand and empathize with the other side of the issue.

If you are in a moderator role, you'll need to corral the discussion if it goes "off track." It is very easy for emotion to creep in from all parties. When that happens, people start to express their opinions or interpretations of the facts with more spirit and color, which sends the discussion down the wrong track. Gently remind the group what the objective is and refocus conversation toward the sharing of the facts and not assigning blame.

Own it

If you are one of the parties involved in the conflict, take full ownership of mistakes that you made that contributed to the conflict. Mistakes are inevitable. The most important thing is how you respond to those mistakes. Owning your portion demonstrates humility and a commitment to moving the resolution process forward. When you need to, acknowledge the mistake you made and how it impacted others. Do not shortchange how it impacted them. This kind of understanding and acknowledgment is critical in the healing process.

When explaining the mistakes, outline how the factors at play contributed to your misstep to help the other person(s) understand that it was not a case of you wanting to "wrong" them. Be careful not to make excuses and give the appearance of shirking the role you played in the conflict. Just outline the facts and circumstances that helped drive you toward your mistake.

Test your hypothesis

Once each party has had a chance to be heard and share their side of the story, it is appropriate to move the process forward. Be cautious and do not rush the fact-finding part of the process. Once all the facts have been stated and everyone has had an opportunity to share, then proceed by stating your interpretation of the situation based on the facts as you see them. Acknowledge that this is your interpretation. When highlighting mistakes or breakdowns, acknowledge that mistakes are natural and helpful to growth if addressed properly. Take ownership of your contributions to the issues.

Then provide the other parties with the opportunity to share their interpretation. You can open the discussion by asking if anyone has a different interpretation or if they agree with your view and/or have anything to add.

Take action and make a commitment

Collaborate with the involved parties to make a joint commitment on next steps and how to handle the situation differently next time. This may require you to propose potential solutions to get the dialogue moving forward. It helps to explain the pros and cons of each of your proposed solutions. Take a matter-of-fact approach here, because it will help to steer the objections or discussion to a more logical place rather than an emotional one. Again, it is important to make sure all parties contribute to this joint resolution. If even a single party does not feel ownership in the resolution, then you have not fully rectified the issue. Bring the discussion back to those holdout individuals by asking them for their thoughts on how to improve the situation and resolution.

These are emotional circumstances, and the way to resolution may not follow a logical and linear path. As the individual leading the process, you will need to do everything you can to include others so as to avoid any suspicions that you are pushing your own agenda.

Finding a remedy for the issue is only one part of the equation. Everyone will feel better about the proposed solution if each party commits to what they are going to do moving forward, to avoid making the same mistake again.

Follow through and rebuild

The most important piece in rebuilding the relationship and establishing trust is to follow through on commitments when defining a resolution. Often this is the most neglected part of the process. Sure, everyone gets to a better place and makes commitments to change, but then they fail to follow through. Do this and the trust is irrevocably broken; you will have almost no chance at salvaging a working relationship. That is why it is hypercritical to follow through on your commitments and help others to do so when possible. This is step one in your reestablishing trust and getting the relationships to a better place. This trust will be the foundation of your relationship moving forward. When done correctly, you will have even stronger relationships than you did before the problems.

Take extra steps to over-communicate in the early stages of the follow-through. Show there is a reason for others to trust again. This also helps to ensure you are getting credit for your follow-through, in case those commitments are not easily seen.

Demonstrate that you are committed to the agreed-upon course of action. This means scheduling a follow-up meeting after a couple of weeks to see how things are going with the other party. Ask them how things are going from their end and if there is anything additional that would help to keep the process moving forward and improve the working relationship. Also in the meeting, share what you have been doing to help thus far.

Don't worry about being proficient at conflict resolution out of the gate. Each situation is unique and will require different methods to corral the discussion and the emotions toward a positive result. Thus, it is easy to see that this is a skill that requires a great deal of practice. With a solid framework to manage conflict and a desire to get better at it, you will be well positioned to develop a strong skill for resolving conflict. As you improve your ability to resolve conflict, you will notice a material growth in interpersonal relationships with your coworkers and overall effectiveness at getting things done in the office.

INFLUENCING OTHERS WITH FINESSE

The ability to influence others is one of the most useful skills an employee can have. Every day in the workplace your skills of persuasion will be put to the test. Even if you are not a direct manager of a team member, you are required to persuade and compel your team members and coworkers to act. To be clear, this is not manipulation; this is persuading and encouraging participation when you are meeting unnecessary resistance. Influencing others is about how to make it appealing for them to act in a manner that is best for all parties. Like a lot of different tools or skills, this is one that can be abused. You will have to be careful to avoid stepping into manipulation territory. In the short term, that type of manipulation may benefit you, but in the long term you will pay a great price in terms of your credibility and ethics.

Let's walk through a primer on how to be more effective at influencing

others. For a deeper dive, read some of the excellent books available on persuasion and implementing change. One of my favorites, which has been significant in my career, is *Influence: The Psychology of Persuasion* by Robert Cialdini.

What's my purpose?

Starting out, when you engage someone else, make sure to paint a clear picture of
what the future would look like with this desired change or behavior. The future
picture that you are painting becomes more powerful when you use examples of
other successful organizations and individuals who have taken on this change or
activity. This gives credibility and validation to your ideas. We are still creatures of
a herd mentality (we believe there is safety in numbers). This can help people get
over their fear, because they know this is a path that has been taken before. Also, a
number of studies have found that people are more willing to oblige if they understand the purpose behind the request. Help them understand the full picture, and
it will help you to compel the other person to act in a productive manner.

WIIIFM: What is in it for me?

Always be thinking in terms of what is in it for me—or WIIIFM—for the other
person. By nature, we have some selfish tendencies. Selfishness is hard-coded into
us as an instinct that has helped us survive as a species. So, when presenting your
ideas or making a request, think about how they can improve the work life of the
other person. Will it make their job easier? Will it save them time in the future?
Tying the request to WIIIFM will help you gain traction on securing buy-in.

Make it simple

It helps to take a simple and direct approach to presenting these ideas to others.
People will often dance around the point when making a request, and then

it becomes a long and uncomfortable conversation for both people involved. Additionally, the long and drawn-out presentation can overcomplicate things (or at least give an overly complex impression). Be clear and concise to ensure that the other person fully grasps your vision and request.

Validate!

Find ways to validate your request. This could come in the form of examples of other companies or departments who have had success with this approach, or even the use of data and statistics if possible. Data and statistics serve as an independent validation of your thoughts. The more reputable the source, the stronger the validation.

Demonstrate that you have done your homework and validate the merit of your ideas. This will help your credibility; people will see that this has been well-thought-out and is not a knee-jerk response or a half-baked idea.

Remove the fog

If you have been successful securing buy-in logically and emotionally, you then need to demystify the next steps. Often people will resist change or action because they are unable to fully comprehend what the next steps are. The mystery around what is next can make the task seem unnecessarily daunting.

How many times have you delayed a perceived difficult task or errand because you thought it was going to be a long, arduous process? Often, I wager. And I imagine many times when you finally confronted that task it was not nearly as difficult as you built it up to be in your mind. The unknown created an irrational fear. That thought process makes the task or the path to accomplish the task seem far more challenging than it really is. These fears can be removed for a good portion of your audience if you outline next steps and draw a road map of the path that will be taken.

Do nice things

Your requests will receive a much higher rate of acceptance if you establish strong relationships with coworkers early on. As I mentioned earlier in the book, establishing strong relationships throughout the organization will yield great dividends. Now it is time to reap the benefits. People are more likely to accommodate a request from someone they like and know.

Take the time to get to know people inside and outside your department. Learn about each person, and understand their likes and dislikes.

Do nice things. People generally like others who do nice things. Additionally, these efforts equate to deposits in your social checking account with this person. Most people will feel a sense of indebtedness, or obligation, to do something nice for someone who has done something nice for them.

Be a good coworker and put in the effort to help others whenever the opportunity presents itself. Modeling the ideal behavior is a powerful tool of influence.

Make it feel urgent

Advertisers are notorious for using this principle. Have you ever heard the term "while supplies last" or "for a limited time only"? Of course you have. This is a subtle way of creating scarcity and compelling us to act quickly. They are suggesting that if you don't act now, you will miss out. Playing on the fear of missing out is a powerful way of getting people to act. The thought of missing out drives us crazy. That is why you will see intentionally long lines to get into clubs, while supplies last, only two seats left at this price . . . you get the idea.

Are there ways for you to emphasize a limited time or availability in your request to encourage a sense of urgency? A perfect example is to use a compelling event like a board meeting or a conference as the deadline for the team to complete a request or project.

Your ability to influence others is something you will use every day at work, regardless of your level in the organization. A common misconception is that once you get to the point of leading teams or departments you can dictate what needs to happen. You may have the authority; however, if you constantly use the dictator approach you will quickly alienate your team. Strong leaders influence and encourage their teams to perform. A refined ability to influence others is the hallmark of those who are successful in the workplace.

DO YOU SPEAK "AWARENESS"?

Awareness is a second language that all aspiring leaders need to be fluent in. Your surroundings can serve as a barometer of the lay of the land, provide early warning signs of missteps or contention, identify conflict, and contribute to the general feeling of how things are going. Throughout the day, large quantities of information are being expressed by others with their nonverbals and actions, and in most cases they go unnoticed. Those who are more astute and aware of this other language extract more information than relying on the words spoken as the sole information source allows. Few in the workplace do this well, so this provides you with a huge advantage over the majority of your peers.

Before you can be effectively aware, you must become more familiar with yourself. Gain a firm understanding of who you are and how you look at the world. This shapes the lens through which you view things, and is the foundational element to successfully understanding what is going on around you at a deeper level. Some tips follow.

Know thyself

Your life experience is the lens through which you are looking at everything. Your life experiences (positive and negative) will shape how you interpret your environment. These experiences create biases that you will use to tell a story. The mind packages information into bite-size chunks and categorizes information. It simplifies and shortcuts into biases, or what you believe to be norms based on a set of experiences. These biases can help you confirm things quickly, but they can also mislead you and drive you to an inaccurate conclusion. That is why it is vital to firmly understand who you are and how you view the world. Let's see how to gain a better understanding of your "default" settings, to empower you to better assess the stories you are telling yourself.

- What are your strengths and weaknesses?

We often discount our strengths and will assume most people have these strengths. As for weaknesses, it is easy for us to be impressed by others who excel at one of our weaknesses because we have internalized that activity as being extremely difficult. Both examples show how our internal narrative can be distorted by our strengths and weaknesses.

- What are your core values?

These are the things that you firmly believe in and were likely instilled in you by your parents and early environment.

- What are your pet peeves?

What about big pet peeves, or things that upset you easily? Take note of them, because when these, along with your core values, are violated, it is easier for you to potentially overreact.

- What are characteristics and behaviors of a good friend?

Your answer here will be very telling. This will help you understand how you believe people should treat each other. Your values here will serve as the barometer of judging the severity of missteps or the merit of positive activities when it comes to interpersonal relationships.

- What do you do in your free time?

Are there sports or hobbies that you are passionate about? What are your political leanings and religious beliefs? These are powerful con-texts that will shape how you interpret your environment and judge actions. Spend a fair amount of time understanding these beliefs and determining why you hold them.

- Your life experiences shape how you view the world and each interaction.

  If you bring a certain partiality to the table it will impair how you assess the situation. It will be driven by your sample size, which can be flawed due to the lack of statistical significance. As you assess your past, think about any traumatic experiences you encountered while growing up. Are there things in your past that left a scar (liter-ally or figuratively)? Things like relationships gone wrong, or public failures? These traumatic experiences have a way of sticking with us and forever changing our outlook and responses.

These are just a few areas for you to think about as you begin your journey of self-discovery. By no means is this intended to be a comprehensive list. The above exercise is something that you should take time to digest and not try to do all at once. Spreading the exercise out over time will help you gain a deeper understanding of why you are the person you are. The intent is to get you thinking about the types of things that can influence how you perceive your environment, and to help you to start asking questions about why you feel a certain way or hold a certain belief, because it is likely due to a past experience.

Your lens

As you gain a better understanding of what shapes your views, start to look at how they manifest in your decisions and assessments. The next level of under-standing and internal awareness is how you arrive at certain conclusions.

Examine the thought process that led to your conclusion on a given event. Push yourself to deeply understand what is behind your conclusion or judgment. It can be helpful to take the approach of a three-year-old. At that age, children tend to repeatedly ask, "Why?" If you do the same and genuinely answer several whys, you are likely to reach the core of the matter.

Next, determine if there were facts that you weighted heavily and other facts that you discounted. Why is that? What past experiences are you using to develop your theory? To determine the validity of your sample size, are those experiences you are drawing from things that have occurred once or many times in different situations and environments?

When people are introduced into the equation, you will need to scrutinize how your preconceived notions of them are impacting your analysis. How do you feel about this individual? Are there any negative experiences or feelings that could be clouding your judgment? This is one of the most difficult areas of the assessment. Our mind wants us to shortcut and assign a good or bad status to people.

For the most part, though, people are not wholly good or bad. Generally, we are walking contradictions that will make mistakes, have lapses in judgment, do great things, etc. This does not mean you should dismiss a hunch because someone has a track record that is predominantly good or bad. Instead, look at the facts to ensure that you are making your decision based on all of the information available—and not just a reputation. Relying solely on reputation can be dangerous and will lead to wrongful accusations and poor decisions.

Take note of your tendencies and try to identify consistent themes that shape your conclusions. This level of awareness will help you make more informed decisions and limit your biases from misleading you.

YOUR SITUATION

Having a strong understanding of yourself will aid you in your decision-making process. However, there are ever-changing elements that have a major impact and can disrupt your evaluation process. They are the situational elements at play.

Any time you are evaluating or trying to understand why a certain decision was made (by yourself or someone else), take time to assess and understand the situation. Acknowledge how these situational factors will impact your view and others, because it can dramatically shift what you think is right or wrong.

Internally understand what your emotional state is, and make best efforts to do the same for the other person(s) involved. A person who is stressed or has been working long hours to complete a large project will likely be more susceptible to irritability, have a shorter fuse, and be more likely to jump to negative conclusions. If you are upset with someone for making a rash decision, consider what is going on around them that could have shaped it. Maybe they felt as though they were under a mountain of stress and made a quick, less-than-rational decision. That level of understanding and empathy will aid you in making better decisions and engaging others when corrective action is necessary.

As you look outside of yourself and others, take inventory of what factors are at play around the situation. Is it a high-stress situation with tight deadlines looming? Or is it a low-stress, walk-in-the-park environment? These external factors are not intended to be an excuse for poor behavior; they are data points for you to make sense of. They should help you to come to more informed conclusions and decisions by enhancing your judgment.

READING THE ROOM

Understanding what is going on around you in real time is a useful skill set. Collecting data points as you operate allows you to adjust on the fly and make modifications that can enhance your overall effectiveness.

This is difficult to do, but practice over time will help you strengthen your ability to read and react in a constructive manner. The following sections should help you to understand the nonverbals and potential undercurrents at play when you are working a room.

Take inventory

As you enter a room, take an initial inventory of what is going on and the emotional state of the room collectively and individually. Just like reading body language, evaluate the current state and how that compares to baseline norms.

This means paying attention to how everyone is positioned in the room as you enter or as they enter. Is it a welcoming room, or is it tight? How do you know? Look for signs of people talking to each other and smiling, indicating a cordial environment, versus heads down in the notes or on their phones, not looking at each other nor engaging in small talk. How does this compare to normal behavior? If it is different, something may be afoot.

When you enter the room, do you notice a shift, positive or negative? Do the conversations come to a screeching halt (bad sign), or are you greeted with warm, genuine smiles? A genuine smile causes the skin around the outsides of the eyes to wrinkle up. What does your gut say? Does it feel like you are welcome in this room or that the good time stopped now that you entered? When others greet you, do they square up and point their whole body directly at you (shoulders, hips, and feet), or do they give you a head-turn greeting instead? Squaring up is a sign of comfort and like, while the latter can be a sign that they are not overjoyed to see you. Take note of who makes eye contact or repositions their body to welcome you into the room. These are likely friendlies.

On the other hand, take note of people who do the opposite—the ones who do not acknowledge your entrance into the room and physically turn away or inward to avoid welcoming you to the room. You will need to work on getting them on your side.

Paying attention to these positive and negative undercurrents will help you perform at your best.

Warm up the room

In a room that is less welcoming, when the attendees have their guards up, it may take extra effort in small talk to warm things up before jumping into business. In sales presentations especially, people's inner skeptic comes out. Spend a few minutes on the appropriate pre-work discussion topics that individuals in the room can connect with, topics that you know are of interest to multiple attendees in the room, or ice breaker exercises.

Stating the obvious here, politics and religion are not appropriate topics to touch on. Those are polarizing subjects, and you will lose a healthy percentage of the room if you introduce those topics into the discussion.

As the small talk progresses, pay attention to the body language in the room. Do you see shoulders dropping and people opening up their body language (uncrossing of arms and legs) and smiling? Then it is time to get rolling, as you have officially "broken the ice." While a few minutes of small talk is appropriate, if it expands beyond that, it has diminishing returns, and you could be viewed as not taking the meeting seriously or not respecting the others' time.

Watch out for shifts

Regardless of whether you are presenting or not, always be engaged with the speaker and the audience. While you are presenting, take note of any immediate shifts in mood or body language of an attendee. If you are an attendee of the meeting, your primary focus should be directed at the speaker; but also, every few minutes glance around the room to gauge how others are engaging and if there is a dramatic shift in mood of any of the individuals. Look for the following:

- A dramatic shift in the status quo, like transitioning from a smile to a frown, or vice versa.
- Did you or a speaker upset someone? Was there physical movement away from you or away from the table? Crossing of the arms or legs to create a barrier is another potential sign of displeasure. A person who has their arms crossed or has squared their shoulders away from you is in a protective pose. This could mean that they have not warmed up to you or the group yet. It could also mean you or the speaker made

them feel uncomfortable and they feel the need to "protect" themselves. Here are a few other defensive tells:

- Legs crossed away from the person
- Building barriers
- Adding a chair or a piece of furniture in between you during the conversation
- Leaning/angling away
- Pushing away or back from the table

- Also take note of the positive reactions. Do you see smiling and positive nonverbals like nodding along and leaning toward you, or solid eye contact? Then it is likely you or the speaker are hitting the mark.

- Is an audience member disengaged? Signs that a person is disinterested or not paying attention to you include gazing around the room or out a window, looking at their phone, and angling their body away from you as you speak. Subtly try to engage them and pull them back into the conversation with a question or referring to them by name in your presentation.

- Are you or a speaker rambling on too long and losing the audience? If you start to see more signs of disengagement—if they're looking at their watches or phones for the time, or even start to have their feet and bodies angled toward the door—you may be guilty. If you see this, act to reengage the group by upping your energy, encouraging more interactivity with the audience, or even trimming down the rest of your presentation to get to the close quicker.

If you see a positive or negative change, identify what you said that could have triggered that response. If it was a negative response, honestly assess what you could have said that was offensive, misinterpreted, or touched a sore subject. Try to take corrective measures like clarifying your point or providing additional context.

Just like reading body language, try to take in the contextual clues at your disposal to round out the picture. Is someone checking their phone and growing more upset every time they check it? Their change in body language may not be about you. There is a chance that something going on outside of the room is causing the issue. However, you will still have a potential ticking time bomb at the table. You need to stay aware and do your best to ensure you don't become the focus of their frustration, ultimately derailing your presentation.

When you engage a disengaged participant, you may see positive responses and body-language shifts in a good way, or you could exacerbate the situation. If you start to engage individuals who appear disengaged and their body language gets worse or starts to show signs of anxiousness, you should likely stop trying to engage those individuals. Some common signs of anxiousness are fidgeting with fingers, clothing, or pens, and constantly looking at their phone, watch, or a clock. Often you will see some calming behaviors accompanying this, like wiping their hands on their thighs or taking deep breaths, as signs of individuals trying to pacify their discomfort.

We have barely scratched the surface on the information that you can obtain while paying attention to how others respond. Start with these basics and practice regularly to hone your skills and to collect the additional data points that many are oblivious to.

Most people understand the basics of managing relationships—be courteous, exhibit good manners, and show gratitude. These are great foundational elements. However, if you desire more in your career, you will need to leverage advanced tactics to create deeper and richer workplace relationships with your customers.

Advanced tactics will help you overcome challenges that the average employee cannot. They lead to enhanced productivity and strength in your working relationships throughout the organization.

As you likely have learned in your career thus far, in business it is difficult to quantify the performance of individuals. Master these skills, and not only will you accomplish more, but you will also establish deep and meaningful relationships with your customers. You'll be viewed in a positive light when you are being evaluated, and you'll have put yourself and your brand in the best position to advance.

IDEAS IN ACTION

▸ Honest conversations come from a well-intended place and provide feedback and opportunities for improvement that will help the other person.

▸ The content of honest conversations focuses on the performance and behaviors with a pragmatic emphasis, not on the other person and their ego.

▸ When done correctly with positive intent and the right focus, the feedback helps the person receiving it to improve and ultimately deepens the relationship between the two parties involved.

▸ The elements behind conflict resolution: removing emotion, preparation, respect, safety, open discussion, ownership, test your hypothesis, take action, and follow through.

▸ Your ability to influence others is something you will use every day at work, regardless of level. A common misconception is that once you lead teams or departments you can merely dictate what needs to happen.

▸ Your surroundings can serve as a barometer of the lay of the land, provide early warning signs of missteps or contention, identify conflict, and give a general feeling of how things are going.

▸ Throughout the day, large quantities of information are being expressed by others through nonverbal cues and actions, and in most cases they go unnoticed.

Get Busy Now

Now that you are equipped with new knowledge on how to improve your career prospects, what are you going to do with it? What changes are you going to make? The key to any learning exercise is to put that knowledge to work efficiently. If you wait a few days, those days end up turning into weeks. As each week passes, you are further removed from the content and remembering less and less of it.

High achievers put their newfound knowledge into practice as soon as possible. That is why if you want to maximize the benefit from the knowledge and practices you have obtained from this book, you will need to chart out your plan of attack to implement it immediately.

As you start to practice and polish your skills, do not expect an overnight change. Improvement takes time. Stay persistent and focused on your objectives. Your career and the evolution of your skills are a marathon. Steady and consistent progress will yield the greatest returns. Inevitably you will face many bumps in the road and obstacles on your journey.

Mistakes and miscues have been a very important part of my personal and professional growth. My short professional baseball career is a great example of this. I molded myself into a pitcher with little high school experience and essentially no college playing time. (I briefly walked on as a senior.) Every night after a ten-to-twelve-hour day at my office job, I would work on my pitching development plan. I did not miss an opportunity to pursue my dream. It did not matter if there was snow on the ground, I would get my workout in. I would run through simulated bullpen sessions by throwing against an elementary school brick wall (with a strike zone painted on it), because I could not find someone foolish enough to catch my bullpen sessions during the cold nights of a Chicago winter. I worked out constantly, read everything I could on pitching, and took pitching lessons from an instructor who typically worked with young kids. The goal was simple: to get a little bit better each day. I did that over a period of several years.

As I progressed, I went to every open tryout I could and was cut from every team (including independent leagues). Those failures did not deter me. I kept working and looking for that next opportunity to display my skills. With a ton of hard work and some good fortune, I secured a workout with the New York Mets. My preparation finally paid off as I dazzled them in my workout and was signed the next day. My transition from the business world to professional baseball was a rapid one. I was in an office on a Friday and in spring training on Monday.

My time in professional baseball was marked by several key mistakes. I assumed that the organization would have a plan for my development, just as they would with all players. Because of my lack of experience, I thought I was different, and that they would nurture me accordingly. I couldn't have been more wrong. I struggled, trying to find a direction for the development of my skills and my baseball career.

Another mistake I made was that I became focused on mechanics during my first season. *Obsessed* may be a better way to put it. This singular focus compromised my development in the following ways:

- I became very rigid, because I was overthinking each and every movement in games when I should have been focused on competing.
- I completely neglected other areas of my development.
- I lacked confidence in a major way because of what I believed was a deficiency in my past experiences compared to everyone else in pro ball.
- The focus on my mechanics and the constant change drew my attention away from the development of my pitches and their effectiveness.

These things, coupled with a few health challenges (hip and shoulder issues), made my professional career a rather short one. I am often asked if I miss playing or wish I was still playing. And the answer is yes, of course. But despite the challenges, I look back at my time very fondly. I was given a gift: a chance to play professional baseball, even though it appeared to be a long shot at best when I started the pursuit of my dream. I put my best effort forth and learned critical lessons about organizations and myself that have helped propel every aspect of my personal and professional life since.

My rapid ascent through the business ranks can in many ways be attributed to my baseball miscues. Since then, I have never assumed that any person or organization, other than myself, is responsible for my development. I personally own that. I made sure that the first skill I built up was my confidence, and that I embodied and projected self-belief. It has served me well. An early mentor (and now a friend) of mine summed it up quite well: "Lukas, you have accomplished and tackled many business challenges that, at the time, you were not even remotely qualified to take on."

I take that as a huge compliment. It means that my preparation and self-belief helped to propel me through challenges that I lacked experience with. Thank you, baseball, and my previous failures.

That's the funny thing about failing. Most of us are taught at an early age to be afraid to fail. We don't want to look foolish. While I am not advocating to purposely try to fail, just don't be afraid of it. That fear will cripple your growth. Mistakes and miscues can help you:

- Learn great lessons
- Remove the fear of tripping up and allow you to try things that you never would have attempted before
- Find out where the limits are
- Find a greater hunger to succeed

Once you embrace the power that can be derived from failing, you become truly powerful. You welcome the formation of a growth mind-set. A growth mind-set is one that approaches every situation, challenge, and project as an opportunity to improve. An example of this mind-set is athletes in action sports, because you can clearly see the physical manifestation of the power of persistence. Do you think that motor-sports star Travis Pastrana goes out there and on his first attempt at a new trick, like a double backflip on a motorcycle, lands it clean? Think again. There are plenty of failures and injuries behind the scenes. Do a search online for "Travis Pastrana injuries," and they will blow your mind.

His list of injuries is a scary experience to look at, and I don't understand how he is still functioning at the level he is. I digress. Every time he attempts and fails he learns something (and probably hurts himself). But he is not deterred. It makes him successful, that ability to power through every fall and failure, and push the limits of his capabilities. The power of perseverance, the ability to dust yourself off and continue to attack without deterrence, is incredible.

Ordinary people accomplish enormous goals by demonstrating grit and commitment in the face of repeated failures. If you stick to your purpose through difficult times, often you will be able to tap into the deepest parts of your potential.

The most common pitfall that trips up individuals is to look at every situation, challenge, or test in terms of passing or failing. That mind-set simply labels oneself a winner or a loser. The flaw in this approach is that it prematurely stunts the development journey by allowing the individual to ignore valuable feedback from the activity. The next time a person with the pass/fail mind-set is confronted with a similar situation, they are less likely to improve. Those who approach every test, activity, or project with a growth mind-set will continuously benefit and prosper, while those who see it as pass or fail will never learn or move forward.

Guess what—you will make many mistakes in your career as you develop your skills. It can be the best way to learn. When you make a mistake, it sticks with you. Like a child who touches a hot stove—he only has to do that once to learn from his mistake. So it is in careers: Good workers learn from their mistakes and grow. But the great ones pull from an even bigger pool of learning opportunities—and learn from the mistakes of others.

Don't be deterred by the challenges that confront you in your career. There is a remarkable amount of talent buried inside you. To fully realize it, you must be dedicated and persistent enough to dig deep and unearth it.

Resources

OBJECTIVE PLANNING SHEET

My Mission Statement _____
_____
_____

My Objective for the next 3 months _____
_____
_____

Due Date _____

Tactically, here is what I need to do to accomplish my objectives:

Tactical Item/Milestone	Date and Time of When I Will Start	Due Date

I will track my progress toward my objective through _____

on the following days _____

I will reward myself with _____

for accomplishing this objective by the due date.

My Objective for the next 6 months _____

_____

_____

_____

Due Date _____

Tactically, here is what I need to do to accomplish my objectives:

Tactical Item/Milestone	Date and Time of When I Will Start	Due Date

I will track my progress toward my objective through _____

on the following days _____

I will reward myself with _____

for accomplishing this objective by the due date.

My Objective for the next 12 months _____

_____

_____

_____

Due Date _____

Tactically, here is what I need to do to accomplish my objectives:

Tactical Item/Milestone	Date and Time of When I Will Start	Due Date

I will track my progress toward my objective through _____

on the following days _____

I will reward myself with _____

for accomplishing this objective by the due date.

My Objective for the next 36 months _____

_____

_____

_____

Due Date _____

Tactically, here is what I need to do to accomplish my objectives:

Tactical Item/Milestone	Date and Time of When I Will Start	Due Date

I will track my progress toward my objective through _____

on the following days _____

I will reward myself with _____

for accomplishing this objective by the due date.

360 Review—
Colleague Feedback Form

REVIEW PERIOD: _____

Please take a few minutes to answer the following questions, as honestly as you can, regarding your work with me over the past year. When possible, provide specific examples that have shaped your feedback.

Feedback from you and others will be considered as I prioritize my professional development opportunities for improvement. Your individual feedback will be confidential.

Thank you in advance for your time. Please email the completed form to me by _____.

Your Name:

What strengths and skills do you believe I have displayed in my overall performance?
(e.g., focus on business results, teamwork, innovation/initiative, judgment, commitment, and leadership appropriate to position responsibilities)

What things might I do more of or less of to be even more effective in my current role?
(recognizing there are things everyone might do to continuously enhance their performance)

What additional knowledge or skills would you recommend I acquire to enhance my performance?

What additional knowledge or skills do you see as necessary for me to progress to the next level in my career?

Please rate my overall performance: (check one)

☐ 5-Far Exceeds

☐ 4-Exceeds

☐ 3-Fully Performing

☐ 2-Meets Some

☐ 1-Does Not Meet

Please comment regarding rating/provide examples:

Moving forward, what could I do to work more effectively with you?

Additional Comments:

Top Interview Questions
I Ask Candidates

1. Tell me about your career and what has brought you to this point.

2. What did you enjoy most and least about your last role?

3. What are you most proud of?

4. If money was not an issue but you were still required to work, what would you do?

5. What are you looking for in your next role?

6. What kind of environment are you looking for in your next company?

7. What motivates you?

8. Role-based questions to gauge the level of the candidate's competence in key skills required for the role.

   a. Share with me a time when you . . .

   b. Walk me through your approach for . . .

9. How would your manager and coworkers describe their experience working with you?

10. How do you like to engage and communicate with your coworkers?

About the Author

LUKAS KRAUSE is driven by a relentless desire to learn, grow, and help others achieve their potential.

As a student of professional development, Lukas has developed, refined, and used the practices contained in this book to go from an entry-level position to the C-suite of an industry leading company in less than ten years. Lukas is the Chief Executive Officer for the Real Property Management franchise system and its portfolio of companies. He is an accomplished executive who has received numerous accolades individually (*Housing Wire* named him *"Real Estate Industry's Rising Star"*) and organizationally (*Forbes* named the business one of the top ten franchises for its investment class).

One of Lukas's proudest accomplishments is his pursuit of a life-long dream of playing professional baseball. After facing rejection repeatedly in his original position as a 1st baseman, his pursuit required him to reinvent himself as a pitcher, a position he had only a handful of experiences with early in high school, while working extra hours at a full-time job after graduating college.

His unconventional path demanded that he put in the unglamorous work each and every night. That meant:

- Spending countless hours throwing against an elementary school wall (even having to shovel snow many times to clear an area for simulated bullpen sessions during the dark cold Chicago winters)
- Extensive weight training
- Getting pitching lessons from an instructor who usually worked with little leaguers
- Reading every single book on pitching he could get his hands on

All these efforts paid off and Lukas' dream became a reality when he signed with the New York Mets and went from an office job on a Friday to spring training on a Monday.

Lukas holds a bachelor's degree in marketing from Indiana University and an Executive MBA from the University of Colorado. He lives in beautiful Park City, Utah, with his talented wife Valerie where he tries his best to enjoy all of the outdoor fun—skiing, hiking, and mountain biking—that mountains offer. Lukas hopes now that after the publishing of this book his parents know what he does for a living (for a stretch there they believed he worked for the CIA because of his extensive travel schedule and the overly complex descriptions of what he was working on).

For additional professional development tools and to keep up with Lukas's public appearances schedule, visit us at TheBusinessofYou.com.